INDIAN RECIPES

Easy and Healthy Traditional Indian Recipes Cookbook for Every Day

(Best of Best Indian Recipes for Lunch and Dinner)

Jeffrey Joyner

Published by Alex Howard

© **Jeffrey Joyner**

All Rights Reserved

Indian Recipes: Easy and Healthy Traditional Indian Recipes Cookbook for Every Day (Best of Best Indian Recipes for Lunch and Dinner)

ISBN 978-1-77485-021-3

All rights reserved. No part of this guide may be reproduced in any form without permission in writing from the publisher except in the case of brief quotations embodied in critical articles or reviews.

Legal & Disclaimer

The information contained in this book is not designed to replace or take the place of any form of medicine or professional medical advice. The information in this book has been provided for educational and entertainment purposes only.

The information contained in this book has been compiled from sources deemed reliable, and it is accurate to the best of the Author's knowledge; however, the Author cannot guarantee its accuracy and validity and cannot be held liable for any errors or omissions. Changes are periodically made to this book. You must consult your doctor or get professional medical advice before using any of the suggested remedies, techniques, or information in this book.

Table of contents

Part 1 1
Introduction 2
Indian Cooking Basics 3
Important Techniques 3
Steaming (Dum) 3
Tempering (Baghar or Tadka) 4
Sautéing (Bhunao) 5
Grilling (Tandoori Cooking) 5
Deep-Frying (Talina) 5
Essential Ingredients 6
Spices and Spice Mixes 6
Ginger-Garlic Paste 6
Souring Agents 7
Thickening Agent 8
How to Cook with Spices 8
Spice Combinations 8
How to Prepare Spices 9
Basic Spices 10
How to Grind and Store Spices 11
Turmeric (Haldi) 12
Chili Powder (Lal Mirch) 13
Cumin (Jeera) 14
Asafetida (Heeng) 14
Mustard Seeds (Sarson) 15
Coriander Seeds (Dhaniya) 15

Making Recipes Slow Cooker Friendly 16
Improvisation and Shortcuts 16
LENTIL RECIPES 18
    Spiced Coconut Lentils 18
    Healthy Lentil Curry 19
    Delicious Black Lentil Curry 21
    Lentil Butternut Squash Curry 22
    Simple Slow Cooker Lentil 23
    Lentil Potato Coconut Curry 24
    Spicy Lentil Stew 25
    Gluten Free Masala Lentils 27
    Flavorful Red Lentils Curry 28
    Cauliflower Lentil Curry 29
    Delicious Tempered Lentils 30
    Lentil Sweet Potato Soup 32
    Potato Red Lentil Curry 34
    Healthy Spinach Lentils 36
    Easy Lentils Rice 38
    Lentil Chicken Vegetable Curry 39
    Healthy Green Lentil Curry 41
    Smokey Lentil Soup 43
    Spinach Coconut Lentil Soup 44
    Spicy Keema Lentils 45
    Creamy Split Pea Curry 46
    Lentil Vegetable Soup 47
    Delicious Lemon Lentils 49
    Tasty Carrot Lentils Soup 50

Lentil Sweet Potato Beans Stew 52
BEANS AND PEAS RECIPES 54
    Healthy Chickpeas and Tofu 54
    Chickpea Pumpkin Lentil Curry 55
    North Indian red Beans 57
    Simple Black Eyed Peas 59
    Tasty Black Eyed Pea Curry 60
    Healthy Green Pea and Cauliflower Korma 61
    Red Beans Bowl 62
    Chickpea Lentil Chili 64
    Red Beans and Lentils 65
    Simple Chickpea Curry 66
    Pea Chickpea Vegetable Curry 67
    Perfect Curried Baked Beans 67
    Red Beans with Bell Pepper 69
    Spicy Black Eyed Peas 69
    Chickpea Coconut Quinoa Curry 70
    Red Beans Cabbage Soup 71
    Gluten Free Chickpea Curry 72
    Vegetarian Chili Bowl 73
    Healthy Turmeric Lentil Bean Chili 75
    Chickpea Kale Sweet Potato Stew 76
    Chickpea Spinach Cauliflower Curry 77
    Spicy Winter Chickpeas 79
    Spicy Curried Chickpeas 81
    Spiced Green Peas Rice 83
    Buttered Peas Rice 84

VEGETABLE RECIPES 85
   Delicious Spiced Potatoes and Cauliflower 85
   Scrumptious Spinach Paneer 86
   Tasty Spinach Potato 87
   Spicy Eggplant Potatoes 88
   Healthy Vegetable Coconut Curry 89
   Easy Whole Cauliflower Curry 90
   Vegetable Curried Rice 92
   Curried Zucchini Eggplant 93
   Flavourful Vegetable Korma 94
   Potato Okra Curry 95
   Delicious Navratan Korma 96
   Slow Cooker Sambar 97
   Creamy Carrot Squash Soup 98
   Yummy Slow Cooked Potatoes 99
   Curried Potatoes 101
   Eggplant Chickpea Curry 104
   Coconut Eggplant Curry 105
   Creamy Cauliflower Soup 106
   Delicious Sweet Potato Curry 107
   Flavorful Vegetable Curry 108
   Delicious Tofu Coconut Curry 109
   Creamy Coconut Pumpkin Curry 111
   Hearty Potato Curry 112
   Mix Vegetable Curry 114
MEAT RECIPES 116
   Tasty Chicken Tikka Masala 116

Delicious Chicken Tandoori 118
Peanut Butter Chicken 119
Spicy Chicken Curry 120
Juicy and Tender Goat Curry 122
Delicious Slow Cooked Beef 123
Simple Beef Curry 125
Easy Curried Chicken 126
Chicken Vegetable Curry 128
Spicy Cauliflower Chicken 130
Yummy Butter Chicken 131
Lamb Curry 133
Chicken Quinoa Curry 135
Delicious Chicken Stew 136
Creamy Coconut Chicken Curry 137
Tasty Chicken Kheema 138
Shredded Lamb 140
Yummy Chicken Soup 141
Sweet Beef Curry 143
Yellow Chicken Curry 144
Spinach Lamb Curry 145
Classic Lamb Curry 146
Easy Lamb Stew 147
Spicy Beef Roast 148
Spicy Beef Stew 150

Part 2 151
Indian best recipes 152
  1. Aloo Palak 152

2. Gobi Manchurian 153

3. Sindhi Saibhaji 155

4. Shahi Paneer 157

5. Potato in Curd Gravy 158

6. Navratan Korma 159

7. Malai Kofta 160

8. Samosa 162

9. Masala Vada 163

10. Hot Kachori 164

11. Spicy Sev 166

12. Pear and Mango Chutney 167

13. Green All-Purpose Chutney 167

14. Sarson ka saag 168

15. Sweet Pongal 169

16. Ulundu vada 170

19. Shrikhand 172

20. Puranpoli 172

21. Patisa (Soan Papdi) 174

22. Coconut Burfi 175

23. Imarti 175

24. Kaju Barfi 176

25. Khajur Burfi or Rolls 177

26. Kalakand (Milk Burfi) 178

27. Badam ka seera 178

28. Carrot Halwa 179

29. Doodhi Halwa 180

30. Chickoo Halwa 180

31. Dal ka seera 181
32. Atte ka seera 182
33. Beetroot Halwa 182
34. Rava (Semolina) Ladoo 183
35. Rossogolla 183
36. Pedhas 184
37. Mava Burfi 185
38. Malai Ladoo 186

Part 1

Introduction

As one of the oldest civilizations still in existence, India contains over a billion people. They are spread out over a diverse set of regions, religions, languages, and even clothing choices. However, this mixture comes together to create the whole of India. Just as the country is varied, so is the food that you can find in the country. Sometimes it's defined by the region as there are some different crops that you will find it specific spots. Sometimes it will depend on the major religion of the area. People that have been in India have also changed the food that they eat as well.

Indian cuisine is loved around the world because of the variety of spices that it uses. Of course, the cuisine is still changing and evolving. The food has become more and more popular which means that the flavors aren't as foreign as they were once before. Dishes like Garam Masala and Haldi are making appearances in kitchens everywhere.

But even as people are falling in love with Indian food, people are running into another issue: time. These dishes are harder to prepare when you are up against the fast moving pace of the rest of your life. People want to still make good food for their family, but it has to be able to work with their life. Many dishes require much more time and attention than we have to give to the dishes we want to make.

In order to help you, we're going to focus on the Dum pukht method of cooking. It is a slow cooking process. It means that you'll be cooking some food in its own juices. It uses fewer spices but keeps the flavors interesting. And these are dishes that you'll be able to put together and then go off and do everything that you need to do. You'll come home to a house that not only smells great but has a dish ready for you already.

Indian Cooking Basics

Everything about an Indian kitchen is wonderful. The spices and sweetness that mix there are incredibly unique and powerful in the modern world. Just the aroma of the spices will make your mouth water. The dish will be even better than the smell. Because of all the flavors and how they mix together, a lot of people have fallen in love with Indian cuisine. While some dishes might seem like they're beyond you, the dishes we are going to go over in this book are going to be well within the range of things that you can do.

Important Techniques

While the common perception is that Indian cuisine and the associated cooking styles are complicated, you'll find that there are some very not complicated techniques that will allow you to get to those complicated flavors. However, regardless of the complicated nature of the dish, there are some basics that you will need to know.

This recipe book is focused on the slow cooker recipes that you are going to be using, but there are still techniques that are going to be important to you. We're breaking them down here because you might face several of the techniques together for the same dish. It can seem intimidating when you're looking at the dish, which is why we're going to go over the basics right now and set you up for future delicious dishes.

Steaming (Dum)

Dum is the name of the technique of cooking a dish in its own steams. In cooking with a slow cooker, you will often be using a variation of this technique. This is accomplished in a slow cooker by putting the lid on top of the slow cooker and allowing none of the steam to really escape.

Dum allows the dish to keep the smell and flavors sealed inside. In the past, they would use wheat flour dough to seal the container and then set the pot on hot coals. There, the dish would cook until it was completed. Obviously, you won't be using the wheat flour dough with our recipes, but it is really interesting to know how the style of cooking was originally done.

Tempering (Baghar or Tadka)

When you use tempering, you're going to seasoning your dish with a hot oil that has spices already in it. This kind of seasoning can happen at the beginning of a recipe or towards the end. It will depend entirely on the dish.

In order to infuse the oil, you will heat the oil until it begins almost smoking. At that point, you'll turn the heat way down, then add the spices. After this, you put the oil in the dish.

There is a little bit of danger that you will need to keep in mind when you are doing this dish. When you add the ingredients to the oil, it is likely that oil will bubble and fly around you. You will need to move quickly and make sure that you are protected from the oil that might splash on you. You'll also want to avoid adding water to this mixture as it will cause the oil to splash and will reduce the flavors of the dish.

Add the ingredients to the oil one at a time to make sure that you're getting the most out of each ingredient. You should work from whole spices to the herbs to the powders.

Sautéing (Bhunao)

This is one of the most common ways of cooking foods in all of Indian cooking. You will saute the ingredients over medium to high heat. You'll have to constantly stir the ingredients while you are going. When you are doing this, you might want to add some water to the ingredients. This will keep them from sticking to the pan while you are cooking them.

This sautéing technique will bring out the best flavors of the ingredients. But you might be uncertain about how long you need to saute things, but you should saute the ingredients until the fat separates from the mixture that you are cooking.

Grilling (Tandoori Cooking)

In the past, cooking in the kitchen has been done in clay ovens which are also known as tandoors. The recipes in this book don't require you to have a tandoor. They have been adjusted to better fit with the grill or oven in your kitchen.

Tandoori cooking can also include some marinating. We have included times in our recipes to make sure that you're getting the most out of the flavors in your dish. You'll definitely want to keep the dishes marinating for as long as possible.

Deep-Frying (Talina)

Deep frying is another well-known way of making dishes in India. Typically people will use a wok or something similar in shape and depth for the oil. In this case, you might feel more comfortable using a deep fryer. There are differing opinions about how you should treat the oil for your deep frying. Common knowledge is using new oil every time. But some people like to reuse the oil. You'll want to let the oil heat up between batches of frying things. This will make sure that everything goes according to plan. You should be using just enough oil for the things that you are trying to fry. Using too much can actually be hard.

Essential Ingredients

When it comes to Indian cooking, there are some common ingredients that you will need to be aware of. They are necessary for every dish and they might be a little bit odd for you. But once you've figured out these different flavors, you'll really be able to make each dish unique and interesting.

Spices and Spice Mixes

There are many spices that are used in Indian dishes. They are found in many forms which means that there are tons of ways to really put them together. With mixes, you'll want to create mixes of spices when you need them. You don't want to have them prepared in advance because you want to make sure that all of the spices are the best they can be. However, if you don't have the time to create the mixes, you'll be able to find premade mixes in Indian grocery stores. You'll have to be very careful with the dates on the package as you want to make sure that you are getting good spices and not old ones.

Ginger-Garlic Paste

This mixture, in particular, is very important in this recipe book. In order to help you get the most out of it, we have included a recipe here so you don't have to search for one on your own. You may also be able to find a paste already mixed in an Indian grocery store. This mixture is a little bit tricky since it can cook quickly and possibly burn. You'll want to have your eyes on it while you are cooking.

Oil

When cooking Indian dishes, you will find that ghee (clarified butter) is one of the most common cooking mediums. However, you may want to use light vegetable oil instead. Ghee can provide a unique flavor to the dishes that you are making. In other areas of India, they also use mustard oil. This particular oil is more pungent and has to be heated up to its smoking point before you use it in the cooking process.

You will not find olive oil used in traditional Indian dishes. Olive oil can cause spices to lose their flavors. As well, olive oil burns more easily and cannot often stand up to the high heat required for Indian dishes.

Souring Agents

Indian dishes require so many different flavors all in one dish. In order to get the sour flavors into a dish, you will need special things to bring in the flavor. You will find that tamarind, lime or lemon juice, tomatoes, vinegar, and sometimes yogurt can be used to make a dish have a slightly sour flavor.

Tamarind and lemon juice can replace one another. If you need a souring agent that isn't wet, you will probably use amchoor or dried mango powder in order to get that flavor.

Tenderizer

In order to tenderize meat, you will often use papaya and yogurt. In this book, we also suggest pineapple as a tenderizer instead of just those two.

Thickening Agent

In order to get the body that you need from the sauces in some dishes, you will find that yogurt, chickpea flour, nut pastes, and onions are used. They can really make a sauce thicker and more appealing.

How to Cook with Spices

Spices are a definitely important part of Indian cooking. There is a lot to know about these spices. Ancient texts will often talk about how they can help the human body, preserve dishes, and add flavor to food. The ancient Indian art of healing, known as Ayurveda, focuses in particular on how food plays into the health and well-being of individuals. The texts say that in a single meal or at least once a day, you should have sweet, salty, tangy, and hot flavors. Flavors like these can be provided by spices.

Spice Combinations

When it comes to using spices, they can provide a complex flavor to seemingly simple dishes. But you also have to know how they work together. While there is no right way to mix spices, playing with spices will allow you to find the mixes that you like the most. If you're new, then you might want to take advantage of the fact that there are premade spice mixtures in Indian grocery stores everywhere. These can also just save you some time.

But when it comes to Indian food, you will want to really pay attention to the spices. There is a learning curve of understanding the flavors when they should be added to dishes, and the order you should add them is incredibly important.

Some of the spices need to be cooked to get the most out of their flavors. There are some spices like cloves and raw green cardamom that can be used raw and as a garnish.

How to Prepare Spices

When you are preparing your spices, you need to make sure that you're doing everything right. There are several different ways to prepare spices, so we'll make sure that you're doing everything the right way.

When using oil or ghee for cooking the spices, you will need to make sure that you're getting the oil hot before you're adding the spices. Hot oil is going to retain the flavors of the spices that you are using. If the oil is cold, then you will not get as much flavor. Ghee can be heated quite hot and it will hold the flavors of spices a little bit better than most oils.

When roasting spices, you'll want to make sure that your skillet is dry. You will also want to make sure that you've gotten the skillet hot before you start adding the spices. You'll have to be prepared to move quickly as some of the spices will heat up quickly and can burn.

Also, make sure that you're making the proper substitutions of ingredients when you're trying to substitute things. Some ingredients like coriander powder cannot be replaced by fresh coriander. If you are uncertain about what can be replaced with what, use the index and we'll help you find the right substitution. You will also find that replacing ground spices instead of whole spices is something that you can easily do. The strength of the flavor goes down when you're using the powder, but that can be good sometimes.

You will want to taste your dishes often to adjust the seasonings that you are adding. You will want to make sure that your dish isn't getting overspiced. When you are starting out, you will struggle a little bit to understand exactly how everything works together. As you learn how the spices work, you will be able to change how you use them in each dish with ease.

Before you start cooking, you'll want to make sure that your spices are ready. Many of these recipes will require your spices to be ready to go one right after the other. So make sure that you have them set up and ready to go for when you need them.

Finally, if you burn your spices, just toss them out. You will not want to add the burned ones because they aren't going to taste good.

Basic Spices

These are the spices that you are going to need if you are cooking a lot of Indian food.

Red chili (powder and whole)
Salt
Coriander (powder and whole)
Cumin seeds
Turmeric
Bay Leaves
Mustard Seeds
Cinnamon
Black peppercorns
Cloves
Black and green cardamom
Mango powder
Carom seeds (also known as ajwain or ajowan)
Dried fenugreek leaves
Tamarind pulp

How to Grind and Store Spices

When using spices, the first thing is making sure that you are using the freshest possible ingredients. You will probably want to replace your spices once a year if you aren't using them all the time. In order to test the freshness of your ingredients, you can smell them. If the spices aren't that smelly, then the spice has probably lost the potency that it once had. This is true for spices that are on their own and it is also true for spices that are mixed.

When you are grinding spices, you can use a mortar and pestle. You can also use a coffee grinder, although you will want to have a coffee grinder that is only for the spices that you are preparing.

When storing spices, you will want to keep them in a cupboard or drawer that is far away from direct sunlight. You will also want to keep things in a glass or plastic containers. This will allow you to see how much of the spice that you have.

You will want to avoid using damp utensils when getting spices from the jar. Keeping moisture away will make sure that the ingredients are lasting as long as possible. Storing ingredients in the fridge can keep them fresher especially if you live in a particularly hot area.

Tools

When it comes to cooking, there a variety of tools that you will need. We will, of course, need a slow cooker for all of the recipes in this book, but there are many more tools that you will need.

A deep pan (preferably nonstick)
Tempering pan also know as Tadke ka bartan (1- to 2-cup capacity specifically for tempering)
Food processor
Blender
Sieve
Spice grinder (mortar and pestle, coffee grinder, etc.)

These tools are going to be the specialty tools that you need. There are other tools that you will need, but most of them will already be in your kitchen.

Masaledani

In every Indian kitchen, there is a masaledani. It is a spice box that contains 5 or 6 of the most basic spices. You'll need these spices a lot when you are cooking. In order to help make them less intimidating, we will be going over the basics of these spices.

Turmeric (Haldi)

This is one spice that you have to have. Regardless of the area of origin, turmeric is going to make an appearance in almost all of the dishes from India. You will find that this spice is very similar to ginger, so it may even look like gingerroot when you are picking it up. Fresh turmeric has a particularly strong flavor, but it is often used in a more mild, ground form. In addition to flavor, turmeric adds color to food. It is even considered the Indian equivalent of saffron.

The yellow color and mild flavor are great, but turmeric can also be used as a preservative. When you're making pickles, you might use salt and turmeric as a way of keeping them good for years after you've dried them in the sun.

This spice is used to color everything from cheese to spice mixes, yogurt to salad dressing. It can also help by reducing inflammation and being used as an antiseptic. When you have a cut or bruise, you may want to rub a paste made from turmeric on it. This mixture will help you. Turmeric and warm milk can be combined to help reduce a fever as well.

Thanks to all of the properties of turmeric, there is a special place in the kitchens and homes of Indians for this spice. It is especially important for Hindu households.

Chili Powder (Lal Mirch)

Chili probably made its way into India when Vasco da Gama, a Portuguese explorer, came to the country. The spice has made its way into many of the dishes. The climate of India actually worked well with chilis and many varieties are grown across the country. Chili powder in Indian is very similar to cayenne pepper. However, unlike other areas, the ground pepper is going to be purely the ground pepper. In other parts of the world, ground pepper is sometimes combined with salt and other spices.

These peppers are going to anywhere from orange to dark red and have quite a bit to them. If you aren't able to stomach the spices, then you might need Kashmiri lal mirch. It is the milder version of chili powder and will have some color that it can add to dishes. Some people will use Kashmiri lal mirch purely for the color that it can give to a dish. Chili powder is useful in almost all dishes as many Indian dishes tend to be on the spicy side.

Cumin (Jeera)

Cumin is another of the common spices. There are several ways that cumin is found. You can find it whole or ground. It also comes in two different forms: black and white. Black cumin, also called royal cumin, is a little bit sweeter. It is also a little bit harder to find than white cumin.

However, cumin, in general, has a warm and earthy flavor. This makes it great for soups and stews. You'll find that when you roast cumin, you will have a good flavor to add to cheese and bread. If you have roasted and ground cumin, then you'll want to add it to raita which is a yogurt-based dip. Cumin can help with your digestion, so you'll find it in the Indian form of lemonade, jal jeera.

Asafetida (Heeng)

Asafetida is a bit strong and can smell a little bit like sulfur. This can make it hard to imagine using, but the odor is something that you will smell all over the entire plant when you are cooking. This spice isn't often found in the west, but Indians use it in many different dishes.

It has a delicious flavor when added to dishes in oil. But you'll find that it has great medicinal properties. It can help with digestive issues. It can also help with lung-related issues and diseases like bronchitis and asthma. When people were a little more superstitious, they would use this spice to keep the evil spirits away from children. There are even some beliefs that it can help with anxiety and alcoholism.

This spice is mainly used for lentil dishes. You only need a pinch and sometimes even less in oil to season a whole dish. This is quite a potent spice.

Mustard Seeds (Sarson)

Mustard is a spice that people know all around the world, but it is very common in India. People will use cooked mustard greens to powdered mustard seeds. The flavors are very common. In the western parts of the world, you'll find that most people use yellow mustard, but black mustard is much more common in India.

Mustard seeds are part of salad dressing, vegetable dishes, and curry. The oil that you can get from mustard seeds is as common as olive oil is in Italy. Mustard oil was used long before vegetable oil made its way into the market, but it isn't just used for cooking. It is also used for body massages as well. The health benefits that you get from the oil are very helpful. It is a long strong tasting, so that might take some time to get used to.

Coriander Seeds (Dhaniya)

This is the last ingredient on our list, but it isn't something that you should forget. The smells of this spice are going to make your kitchen smell amazing. Coriander is known in the US as cilantro, but it is also very common in India. It is used in many sauces and as a garnish.

The fruits of this plant have seeds that have a sweet, citrus flavor and a nutty smell to them. This is a staple in the Indian kitchen. You will be able to buy whole seeds and roast them on your own. After roasting, you will want to crush them to use in other ways. You can also make a powder and use it in curries and things. There are many different ways to use these seeds, but they will always be at home in Indian cuisine.

Making Recipes Slow Cooker Friendly

When it comes to making a recipe work in a slow cooker, many will translate easily. You'll be cooking ingredients in a little bit of liquid for a long period of time. You'll be able to play with these recipes and make them work a slow cooker even when they weren't meant to.

But you'll find that some recipes will be a little bit more difficult. Deep frying food in a slow cooker isn't going to work as well, but braising or stewing recipes are going to work easily.

You will even be able to prepare dried beans in the slow cooker. It will involve a little bit of work since you will have to soak them overnight, but it can work really well and cost you just a little bit less than canned beans. But canned beans can save you a little bit of time in the long run.

Improvisation and Shortcuts

Don't be afraid to put your own spin on things according to your unique tastes and preferences. Every recipe looks a little different in different households, so make sure that you try to take the time to make the recipe your own.

Meat

When cooking meat in a slow cooker, you will not have your meat browned in the cooker. If you want browned meat, then you're going to need to brown it a little bit before you add it to the slow cooker. Just searing the meat or quickly sautéing it will allow it to look brown.

If you are making a stew and need a thick broth, then you can coat the meat in flour. This will not only speed up the sautéing and browning but also help thicken the sauce.

Slow cooking works well with the cheaper, leaner cuts of meat that you need to cook for longer before they become tender. If you are transposing a recipe from oven or stovetop, then you might need to pick a leaner cut of meat that will be better suited to being in the slow cooker.

Make sure that you're not overcooking thing. Poultry tends to cook quickly, so just four hours on low will be enough. Poultry will turn out better when you are using wet ingredients in the slow cooker as well as it will make sure that the lean meat will not dry out.

When you're using a slow cooker, you will save time by not having to marinate your food. The marinating process happens in the slow cooker as it takes hours and hours for the flavors to become part of the dish.

LENTIL RECIPES

Spiced Coconut Lentils

Total Time: 8 hours 20 minutes

Serves: 12

3 cups yellow lentils, Soak for 10 minutes
14 oz coconut milk
1/4 cup cilantro
1 tbsp fresh ginger, peeled and chopped
2 tbsp curry powder
2 tsp ground cumin
2 tsp ground turmeric
1 tsp chili powder
4 chilies, stemmed and seeded
1 large onion, chopped
5 garlic cloves
1/2 tsp sugar
28 oz can tomatoes, diced
Kosher salt

- Rinse lentil and drain well. Add lentil into the slow cooker.
- Add sugar, chili powder, turmeric, cumin, curry powder, ginger, garlic, onion, and Serrano chilies into the food processor and process until mixture becomes a paste. Add into the slow cooker.
- Stir in tomatoes and 6 cups of water.
- Cover slow cooker and cook on low for 8 hours.
- Season with salt and stir well.

- Add coconut milk and stir well. Garnish with cilantro and serve.

Calories 258, Fat 8 g, Carbohydrates 33 g, Sugar 4 g, Protein 13 g, Cholesterol 0 mg

Healthy Lentil Curry

Total Time: 5 hours 10 minutes
Serves: 6

1 1/2 cups green lentils, rinse and drained
3 tbsp tomato paste
14 oz can coconut milk
3 tsp curry powder
1 onion, diced
3 garlic cloves, minced
1 yellow pepper, diced
1/4 tsp pepper
1/2 tsp ground ginger
2 tsp garam masala
2 tsp sugar
2 1/2 cups water
2 tbsp olive oil
1 tsp garlic powder
1 tsp cumin
1 1/2 tsp salt

- Add olive oil, yellow pepper, garlic, and onion into the slow cooker.
- Add lentils into the slow cooker and stir well.
- Add all remaining ingredients and stir well.
- Cover and cook on low for 5 hours.
  - Stir well and serve with rice.

Calories 376, Fat 19 g, Carbohydrates 39 g, Sugar 4 g, Protein 15 g, Cholesterol 0 mg

Delicious Black Lentil Curry

Total Time: 12 hours 15 minutes
Serves: 8

1 cup whole black gram lentils
3 cloves
1 tbsp ginger, chopped
8 garlic cloves, chopped
2 green chilies, cut lengthwise
1 tbsp coriander powder
1/2 tsp turmeric powder
1/2 cup kidney beans
1 bay leaf
1 cinnamon stick
3 cardamom pods
1/2 tsp chili powder
4 tomatoes, diced
1 tsp garam masala
1/4 cup cream
2 tbsp butter
Salt

Soak black lentils and kidney beans in water for overnight.
- Add all ingredients except cream into the slow cooker with 4 cups water and stir well.
- Cover and cook on low for 12 hours.
- Stir well and lightly mash using the back of a spoon.
- Add cream and stir well.
  - Serve and enjoy.

Calories 186, Fat 4 g, Carbohydrates 27 g, Sugar 2 g, Protein 10 g, Cholesterol 9 mg

Lentil Butternut Squash Curry

Total Time: 12 hours 15 minutes
Serves: 8

2 cups red lentils
4 cups butternut squash, cut into cubes
2 tbsp ginger, minced
1 1/2 tsp curry powder
1 tsp ground coriander
1 onion, minced
2 garlic cloves, minced
1 tsp garam masala
1 tsp turmeric
14 oz can coconut milk
19 oz can tomatoes, diced
3 cups vegetable stock
1 tsp ground cumin
1/2 tsp salt

- Add all ingredients into the slow cooker and stir well.
- Cover and cook on low for 8 hours.
  - Serve and enjoy.

Calories 329, Fat 11 g, Carbohydrates 45 g, Sugar 5 g, Protein 15 g, Cholesterol 0 mg

Simple Slow Cooker Lentil

Total Time: 6 hours 15 minutes
Serves: 6

2 cups red lentils, rinsed and drained
1 bay leaf
1 tbsp ground turmeric
1 tbsp fresh ginger, grated
1 medium onion, diced
15 oz can tomatoes, diced
5 cups water
1 tsp fennel seeds
2 tsp mustard seeds
2 tsp cumin seeds
1/4 tsp ground black pepper
1 tsp kosher salt

- Heat pan over medium heat and toast fennel seeds, mustard seeds, and cumin seeds in a pan until fragrant for 2-3 minutes.
- Add toasted spices and remaining all ingredients into the slow cooker and stir well.
- Cover and cook on low for 6 hours.

- Stir well and serve.

Calories 265, Fat 1 g, Carbohydrates 46 g, Sugar 4 g, Protein 18 g, Cholesterol 0 mg

Lentil Potato Coconut Curry

Total Time: 8 hours 15 minutes
Serves: 10

2 cups brown lentils
14 oz can coconut milk
3 cups vegetable broth
15 oz can tomato sauce
15 oz can tomatoes, diced
1/4 tsp ground cloves
3 tbsp curry powder
2 medium carrots, peel and diced
1 sweet potato, peel and diced
2 garlic cloves, minced
1 medium onion, diced

- Add all ingredients except coconut milk into the slow cooker and stir well.
- Cover and cook on low for 8 hours.
    - Stir in coconut milk and serve with rice.

Calories 152, Fat 3 g, Carbohydrates 22 g, Sugar 6 g, Protein 9 g, Cholesterol 0 mg

Spicy Lentil Stew

Total Time: 6 hours 15 minutes
Serves: 8

3 cups red lentils, rinsed and drained
3 1/2 cup tomatoes, crushed
1/2 tbsp black pepper
1/2 tbsp curry powder
1/2 tbsp paprika
1/2 tbsp chili powder
1/2 tbsp garam masala
1/2 tbsp turmeric powder
6 cups vegetable broth
1 onion, diced
2 garlic cloves, minced
3 Serrano chili, diced
2 tbsp cilantro, minced
1 tbsp Creole seasoning
1 tbsp garlic powder
1 tbsp onion powder
1/2 tbsp ginger powder

- Add all ingredients into the slow cooker and stir well.
- Cover and cook on high for 5 hours.
- Uncover the slow cooker and cook for another 50 minutes.
    - Serve and enjoy.

Calories 318, Fat 2 g, Carbohydrates 51 g, Sugar 5 g, Protein 23 g, Cholesterol 0 mg

Gluten Free Masala Lentils

Total Time: 6 hours 10 minutes
Serves: 8

2 1/4 cups brown lentils
4 cups vegetable broth
15 oz can tomatoes, diced
1 medium onion, chopped
3 garlic cloves, minced
1 tbsp fresh ginger, minced
1/4 cup tomato paste
2 tsp tamarind paste
1 tsp maple syrup
1 1/2 tsp garam masala
1 cup coconut milk
3/4 tsp salt

- Add all ingredients except coconut milk into the slow cooker and stir well.
- Cover and cook on low for 6 hours.
  - Stir in coconut milk and serve.

Calories 306, Fat 9 g, Carbohydrates 41 g, Sugar 5 g, Protein 17 g, Cholesterol 0 mg

Flavorful Red Lentils Curry

Total Time: 8 hours 15 minutes
Serves: 16

4 cups brown lentils, rinsed and drained
5 tbsp red curry paste
1 tbsp garam masala
1 1/2 tsp turmeric
2 tsp sugar
1/2 cup coconut milk
29 oz can tomato puree
2 onions, diced
4 garlic cloves, minced
1 tbsp ginger, minced
4 tbsp butter
7 cups water
1 tsp salt

- Add all ingredients except coconut milk into the slow cooker and stir well.
- Cover and cook on low for 8 hours.
- Add coconut milk and stir well.
- Serve with rice and enjoy.

Calories 261, Fat 6 g, Carbohydrates 37 g, Sugar 4 g, Protein 13 g, Cholesterol 8 mg

Cauliflower Lentil Curry

Total Time: 5 hours 15 minutes
Serves: 6

1 cup red lentils
3 cups cauliflower, cut into florets
3 dates, pitted and chopped
2/3 cup coconut milk
1 1/2 tsp turmeric
1 tsp ginger, grated
2 tbsp Thai red curry paste
3 garlic cloves, minced
1/2 onion, chopped
3 cups vegetable broth
1/4 tsp sea salt

- Add all ingredients except coconut milk into the slow cooker and stir well.
- Cover and cook on low for 5 hours.
- Add coconut milk and stir well.
- Serve with rice and enjoy.

Calories 247, Fat 9 g, Carbohydrates 29 g, Sugar 6 g, Protein 12 g, Cholesterol 0 mg

Delicious Tempered Lentils

Total Time: 6 hours 20 minutes
Serves: 6

1 1/2 cups yellow split lentils, rinsed and drained
1/4 cup fresh cilantro, chopped
1 tsp turmeric powder
2 tsp garlic, minced
2 medium tomatoes, chopped
1/2 medium onion, chopped
1 tsp salt
For tempering:
2 tbsp vegetable oil
1/4 tsp chili powder
1/2 tsp coriander powder
1/2 tsp cumin powder
1 garlic cloves, minced
1/2 tsp whole cumin seeds

- Add lentils into the slow cooker with 4 cups water.
- Add turmeric powder, garlic, tomatoes, onion, and salt into the slow cooker and stir well.
- Cover and cook on low for 5 hours.
- Heat vegetable oil in the pan over medium-high heat.
- Once the oil is hot then turn off the heat and add cumin, garlic, and spices. Mix well.

- Stir prepared tempering into the hot lentil.
- Add cilantro and stir well.
- Cook lentils for another 1 hour to blend all flavors.

- Serve hot with rice and enjoy.

Calories 208, Fat 5.2 g, Carbohydrates 28 g, Sugar 1.5 g, Protein 12.7 g, Cholesterol 0 mg

Lentil Sweet Potato Soup

Total Time: 6 hours 20 minutes
Serves: 4

1 1/2 cups brown lentils
1 large sweet potato, cut into 1/2 inch cubes
6 cups vegetable broth
1 cup coconut milk
1/2 tbsp chili paste
1 medium onion, diced
3 garlic cloves, minced
1/2 tbsp ginger, grated
2 tsp ground cumin
1 tsp garam masala
2 tsp lime juice
1/4 cup fresh cilantro, chopped
14 oz can tomatoes, diced
Pepper
Salt

- Add all ingredients except tomatoes and lime juice into the slow cooker and stir well.
- Cover and cook on low for 6 hours.
- Stir in tomatoes and lime juice.
- Cook soup for another 10 minutes to blend the flavors.
- Season with pepper and salt.
    - Serve warm and enjoy.

Calories 395, Fat 17 g, Carbohydrates 54 g, Sugar 11 g, Protein 23 g, Cholesterol 1 mg

Potato Red Lentil Curry

Total Time: 4 hours 15 minutes
Serves: 8

1 cup red lentils, rinsed
2 potatoes, cut into cubed
1 cup brown lentil, rinsed
1 large onion, diced
1/2 tsp turmeric
1/2 tsp cumin seeds, toasted
1 tsp sugar
14 oz can tomato, diced
14 oz can coconut milk
1 tbsp garlic, minced
1 tsp ginger, minced
2 tbsp butter
2 tbsp curry powder
1/2 tsp red pepper flakes

- Add all ingredients except coconut milk into the slow cooker and stir well.
- Add water into the slow cooker to cover lentil mixture.
- Cover and cook on high for 4 hours.
- Add coconut milk and stir well.
- Serve warm and enjoy.

Calories 307, Fat 14 g, Carbohydrates 39 g, Sugar 3 g, Protein 13 g, Cholesterol 8 mg

Healthy Spinach Lentils

Total Time: 4 hours 30 minutes
Serves: 4

1 cup yellow split peas
3 1/2 cups water
10 oz spinach, chopped
1 tsp cumin seeds
1 tbsp fresh ginger, peeled and minced
3 garlic cloves, minced
1 tsp mustard seeds
1 medium onion, diced
15 oz can tomatoes, drained and diced
2 jalapeno pepper, cored and diced
1 tsp turmeric
1/2 tsp coriander
1/4 tsp cayenne
1 tsp salt

- Add all ingredients except spinach into the slow cooker and stir well.
- Cover and cook on high for 4 hours.
- Add spinach and cook for another 20.
- Stir well and serve.

Calories 236, Fat 1.4 g, Carbohydrates 43 g, Sugar 9 g, Protein 16.1 g, Cholesterol 0 mg

Easy Lentils Rice

Total Time: 4 hours 10 minutes
Serves: 6

1/2 cup lentils, rinsed and drained
1 tsp garlic powder
3 1/2 cups vegetable broth
1 tbsp curry powder
1 cup white rice, rinsed and drained
1 onion, diced
1/4 tsp pepper
Salt

- Add all ingredients into the slow cooker and stir well.
- Cover and cook on high for 4 hours.
  - Stir well and serve.

Calories 204, Fat 1.3 g, Carbohydrates 37 g, Sugar 1.7 g, Protein 9.6 g, Cholesterol 0 mg

Lentil Chicken Vegetable Curry

Total Time: 4 hours 20 minutes
Serves: 8

1 lb dried lentils, rinsed and drained
4 cups fresh spinach, chopped
4 cups vegetable broth
1/4 tsp cinnamon
1 1/2 tsp turmeric
1/2 tsp cayenne
1 tbsp curry powder
2 lbs chicken thighs, boneless and cut into pieces
6 garlic cloves, minced
1 small cauliflower head, cut into florets
2 cups carrots, chopped
1 large onion, chopped
1 tsp salt

- Add all ingredients except spinach into the slow cooker and stir well.
- Cover and cook on high for 3 1/2 hours.
- Add spinach and stir well. Cover and cook for another 30 minutes.
    - Stir well and serve with rice.

Calories 473, Fat 10 g, Carbohydrates 42 g, Sugar 4.6 g, Protein 51 g, Cholesterol 101 mg

Healthy Green Lentil Curry

Total Time: 6 hours 15 minutes
Serves: 6

2 cups green lentils, rinsed and drained
3 cups water
6 oz can tomato paste
14 oz can coconut milk
1 tsp cumin
1 tsp curry powder
1/2 tsp ground coriander
1 tsp turmeric
1 tsp vegetable oil
6 garlic cloves, minced
1 large onion, chopped
1 1/4 tsp salt

- Heat oil in the pan over medium heat.
- Add garlic and onion to the pan and sauté for 5 minutes.
- Add cumin, curry powder, coriander, turmeric, and salt and sauté for 1 minute.
- Transfer pan mixture to the slow cooker with remaining all ingredients. Stir well.
- Cover and cook on low for 6 hours.
    - Serve warm with rice and enjoy.

Calories 404, Fat 15.9 g, Carbohydrates 49 g, Sugar 5.9 g, Protein 19.7 g, Cholesterol 0 mg

Smokey Lentil Soup

Total Time: 6 hours 15 minutes
Serves: 6

2 cups red lentils
2 tbsp smoked paprika
2 carrots, chopped
4 garlic cloves, minced
8 cups vegetable broth
1 onion, chopped
3 tbsp fresh parsley, chopped
1/4 cup hulled pumpkin seeds
2 potatoes, peeled and chopped
1/3 cup tomato paste
3 tbsp lemon juice
3 tbsp vegetable oil

- Add lentils, lemon juice, tomato paste, garlic, paprika, carrots, potato, onion, and broth into the slow cooker and stir well.
- Cover and cook on low for 6 hours.
- Meanwhile, in a small bowl, combine together parsley and oil.
- Ladle soup into the bowls and drizzle with parsley and oil mixture.
- Sprinkle pumpkin seeds over the soup.
    - Serve and enjoy.

Calories 474, Fat 9.9 g, Carbohydrates 67.6 g, Sugar 7 g, Protein 25.8 g, Cholesterol 0 mg

Spinach Coconut Lentil Soup

Total Time: 4 hours 45 minutes
Serves: 6

4 cups fresh spinach, chopped
14 oz coconut milk
4 cups vegetable stock
1 1/2 cup red lentils, rinsed and drained
1 tsp ground cinnamon
1/2 tsp garam masala
1 tsp ground turmeric
1 tsp ground coriander seed
1 tsp ground cumin
2 tsp garlic, minced
1 large onion, chopped
1 tbsp vegetable oil
Pepper
Salt

- Heat oil in the pan over medium heat.
- Add onion to the pan and sauté for 5 minutes or until golden brown.
- Add cinnamon, garam masala, turmeric, coriander, cumin, and garlic and cook for 2 minutes.
- Transfer onion-spice mixture into the slow cooker.

- Add lentils and stock into the slow cooker and stir well.
- Cover and cook on low for 4 hours.
- Add coconut milk and spinach. Stir well and cook for another 30 minutes.
- Season with pepper and salt.
- Serve and enjoy.

Calories 368, Fat 20 g, Carbohydrates 37 g, Sugar 5 g, Protein 14.9 g, Cholesterol 0 mg

Spicy Keema Lentils

Total Time: 4 hours 15 minutes
Serves: 4

3 cups green lentils, cooked
1 tsp dried chili flakes
1/2 tsp ground turmeric
2 tsp garam masala
2 tsp ground coriander
2 tsp ground cumin
1 large onion, chopped
3 tbsp fresh ginger, grated
6 garlic cloves, chopped
1 1/2 cup vegetable broth
2 tbsp tamari
1 tsp pepper
1 tsp salt

- Add all ingredients into the slow cooker and stir well.
- Cover and cook on low for 4 hours.

- Stir well and serve.

Calories 206, Fat 0.9 g, Carbohydrates 37 g, Sugar 2 g Protein 15 g, Cholesterol 0 mg

Creamy Split Pea Curry

Total Time: 6 hours 15 minutes
Serves: 6

1 1/2 cups dried split peas
1 cup heavy cream
1/2 tsp ground ginger
2 tsp curry powder
1 tbsp turmeric
1 tbsp green curry paste
3 garlic cloves, minced
1/2 cup onion, diced
15 oz can coconut milk
28 oz can tomatoes, crushed
1 tsp salt

- Add all ingredients except cream into the slow cooker. Stir well.
- Cover and cook on low for 6 hours.
- Add cream and stir well.
  - Serve with rice and enjoy.

Calories 425, Fat 23.8 g, Carbohydrates 42.4 g, Sugar 9 g, Protein 15.5 g, Cholesterol 27 mg

Lentil Vegetable Soup

Total Time: 8 hours 15 minutes
Serves: 8

1 1/2 cups green lentils, rinsed and drained
9 cups vegetable broth
5 peppercorns
3 bay leaves
3 tbsp soy sauce
1 tsp thyme
2 tsp oregano
1 tbsp garlic powder
2 cups corn
4 cups potatoes, diced
3 large carrots, diced
3 large celery stalks, diced
2 medium onion, diced

- Add all ingredients into the slow cooker and mix well.
- Cover and cook on low for 8 hours.
- Discard peppercorns and bay leaves from soup and using blender puree the soup until you get desired texture.
  - Serve hot and enjoy.

Calories 288, Fat 2.6 g, Carbohydrates 49 g, Sugar 6.7 g, Protein 18.5 g, Cholesterol 0 mg

Delicious Lemon Lentils

Total Time: 2 hours 45 minutes
Serves: 8

1 1/2 cups pink lentils
1 tbsp milk
2 tbsp lemon juice
2 Serrano chilies, sliced
1 tbsp fresh ginger, minced
4 garlic cloves, sliced
1 small onion, diced
5 cups water
1 1/2 tsp salt

- Add all ingredients except milk and lemon juice into the slow cooker. Stir well.
- Cover and cook on high for 2 1/2 hours.
- Add lemon juice and stir well.

- Add milk and stir well and serve.

Calories 135, Fat 0.9 g, Carbohydrates 23.4 g, Sugar 0.6 g, Protein 9.4 g, Cholesterol 0 mg

Tasty Carrot Lentils Soup

Total Time: 8 hours 15 minutes
Serves: 8

1/2 cup lentils
2 lbs carrots, peeled and cut into 1-inch pieces
1/2 tsp harissa
1/4 cup maple syrup
1 cup orange juice
4 cups vegetable broth
1 tsp fresh ginger, grated
1/2 tbsp ground cumin
1/2 tbsp curry powder
1 medium onion, peeled and chopped
Pepper
Salt

- Add orange juice, broth, ginger, curry powder, onion, and carrots into the slow cooker and mix well.
- Cover and cook on low for 6 hours.
- Add lentils, harissa, and maple syrup. Stir well and cook on high for another 2 hours.
- Season with pepper and salt.
- Serve and enjoy.

Calories 158, Fat 1.1 g, Carbohydrates 30.6 g Sugar 15.3 g
Protein 7 g, Cholesterol 0 mg

Lentil Sweet Potato Beans Stew

Total Time: 6 hours 30 minutes
Serves: 6

3/4 cup dry lentils, rinsed and drained
3 cups sweet potatoes, cut into 1 inch cubed
1 1/2 cups green beans, cut into pieces
1 1/2 cups baby carrots
1/2 cup plain yogurt
1 3/4 cup vegetable broth
2 garlic cloves, minced
1 tsp fresh ginger, chopped
1 tsp ground cumin
1 tbsp curry powder
2 tbsp vegetable oil
1/4 cup onion, chopped
1/4 tsp black pepper
1/2 tsp salt

- Add lentils, carrots, onion, and sweet potatoes into the slow cooker.
- In a pan, heat oil over medium heat.
- Add garlic, ginger, pepper, cumin, curry powder, and salt and stir for 1 minute. Stir in broth.
- Pour mixture into the slow cooker and mix well.
- Cover and cook on low for 6 hours.
- Turn heat to high and stir in green beans. Cover and cook for another 15 minutes.

- Top with plain yogurt and serve.

Calories 269, Fat 5.9 g, Carbohydrates 43.5 g, Sugar 4.8 g, Protein 10.8 g, Cholesterol 1 mg

BEANS AND PEAS RECIPES

Healthy Chickpeas and Tofu

Total Time: 4 hours 15 minutes
Serves: 6

12 oz firm tofu
15 oz can chickpeas, rinsed and drained
1/8 cup cilantro, chopped
1/2 tsp ground ginger
2 tsp chili powder
1 tbsp curry powder
1 tbsp garam masala
1 cup tomato puree
14 oz can coconut milk
4 garlic cloves, minced
1 medium onion, diced
1 tsp vegetable oil
Pepper
Salt

- Rinse tofu well and pat dry with paper towel. Squeeze out all liquid from tofu and cut tofu into the pieces.
- Heat oil in the saucepan over medium heat.
- Add onion to the pan and sauté for 5 minutes.
- Add garlic and cook for 1 minute.
- Whisk in coconut milk, ginger, chili powder, curry powder, garam masala, tomato puree, pepper, and salt. Cook for 5 minutes.
- Add chickpeas and tofu into the slow cooker.
- Pour pan mixture into the slow cooker.
- Cover and cook on low for 4 hours.
- Garnish with cilantro and serve.

Calories 294, Fat 18.5 g, Carbohydrates 26.2 g, Sugar 3.3 g, Protein 10.8 g, Cholesterol 0 mg

Chickpea Pumpkin Lentil Curry

Total Time: 8 hours 40 minutes
Serves: 6

15 oz can chickpeas, rinsed and drained
1 cup pumpkin puree
1 cup lentils, rinsed and drained
15 oz can coconut milk
1/4 tsp ground cayenne pepper
1 tbsp curry powder
2 cups vegetable broth
2 garlic cloves, minced

1 medium onion, diced
1 tsp kosher salt

- Add all ingredients except coconut milk into the slow cooker and stir well.
- Cover and cook on low for 8 hours.
- Add coconut milk and stir well. Cook for another 30 minutes.

- Serve with rice and enjoy.

Calories 376, Fat 17 g, Carbohydrates 43.5 g, Sugar 3.1 g, Protein 15.7 g, Cholesterol 0 mg

North Indian red Beans

Total Time: 4 hours 15 minutes
Serves: 4

2 cups dry red beans, soak for overnight
2 tbsp cilantro, chopped
1 cup tomato sauce
1 cinnamon stick
1/4 tsp turmeric
1/4 tsp cayenne pepper
1/4 tsp ground coriander
1 tbsp lemon juice
4 garlic cloves, minced
1 tsp ginger, minced
1 medium onion, chopped
1 tsp cumin seeds
1 bay leaf
1 tbsp vegetable oil
1 1/2 tsp salt

- Heat oil in the pan over medium heat.
- Add onion, bay leaf, and cumin seeds into the pan and cook for 5 minutes.
- Add dry spices and lemon juice and stir for 2 minutes.
- Add beans, cinnamon stick, tomato sauce, and salt into the slow cooker.
- Transfer pan mixture into the slow cooker and stir well.

- Cover and cook on high for 4 hours.
- Using spoon lightly mash the red beans it helps to thicken the gravy.
  - Garnish with cilantro and serve.

Calories 376, Fat 4.8 g, Carbohydrates 64.1 g, Sugar 5.9 g, Protein 22.2 g, Cholesterol 0 mg

Simple Black Eyed Peas

Total Time: 6 hours 15 minutes
Serves: 6

1 lb dried black-eyed peas, soak for overnight
1 tsp ground sage
1/8 tsp thyme
1 bay leaf
1 garlic clove, diced
1 small onion, diced
2 cups water
2 cups vegetable broth
1/2 tsp pepper
1 tsp sea salt

- Add all ingredients into the slow cooker and mix well.
- Cover and cook on low for 6 hours.
    - Serve and enjoy.

Calories 203,nFat 0.5 g, Carbohydrates 48.8 g, Sugar 2.8 g, Protein 20.2 g, Cholesterol 0 mg

Tasty Black Eyed Pea Curry

Total Time: 4 hours 15 minutes
Serves: 4

1 cup dried black-eyed peas, soaked for overnight
1 bay leaf
6 garlic cloves, minced
1/2 tsp black pepper
1/4 tsp cayenne
2 tomatoes, chopped
3 cups water
1 tsp ginger, minced
1 tsp turmeric
1/2 tsp cumin seeds
1 large onion, diced
1 tsp garam masala
1 tsp salt

- Add all ingredients into the slow cooker and stir well.
- Cover and cook on high for 4 hours.
  - Stir well and serve.

Calories 128, Fat 0.4 g, Carbohydrates 31.4 g, Sugar 4.3 g, Protein 10.4 gCholesterol 0 mg

Healthy Green Pea and Cauliflower Korma

Total Time: 4 hours 15 minutes
Serves: 4

10 oz green peas
1 cauliflower head, cut into florets
1 cup water
1 1/2 cups coconut milk
1/4 tsp cayenne
1 tsp turmeric
1/4 tsp cumin
2 tsp garam masala
1 medium onion, diced

- Add all ingredients into the slow cooker and stir well.
- Cover and cook on low for 4 hours.
    - Stir well and serve.

Calories 295, Fat 21.9 g, Carbohydrates 21.8 g, Sugar 9.8 g, Protein 7.6 g, Cholesterol 0 mg

Red Beans Bowl

Total Time: 8 hours 15 minutes
Serves: 4

14 oz can kidney beans, drained and rinsed
1/2 tsp garam Masala
1/2 tsp turmeric powder
2 cups onion, chopped
1 tomato, chopped
1/2 inch cinnamon stick
1 bay leaf
2 cloves
1 tsp ginger, minced
5 garlic cloves, minced
1 green chili, chopped
1/2 tbsp cumin seeds
1 tsp cayenne pepper
1 tbsp paprika
Salt

- Add all ingredients except yogurt into the slow cooker and stir well.
- Add 4 cups water and stir to combine.
- Cover and cook on high for 8 hours.
- Using back of spoon mash few beans.
    - Stir well and serve with rice.

Calories 399, Fat 2.1 g, Carbohydrates 72.2 g, Sugar 7.4 g, Protein 25.6 g, Cholesterol 2 mg

Chickpea Lentil Chili

Total Time: 8 hours 15 minutes
Serves: 6

1 cup dried chickpeas, soaked overnight
1/2 cup raisins
2 1/2 cups vegetable broth
1/2 cup water
28 oz can whole tomatoes, undrained and crushed
2 cups sweet potatoes, cut into cubes
1 cup lentils
1/2 tsp chili powder
1/2 tsp ground cinnamon
1/4 tsp ground turmeric
1 cup onion, chopped
5 garlic cloves, minced
1 1/2 tsp ground cumin
1 tsp kosher salt

- Add all ingredients into the slow cooker and stir well.
- Cover and cook on low for 8 hours.
  - Stir well and serve.

Calories 388, Fat 3.3 g, Carbohydrates 73.3 g, Sugar 17.3 g, Protein 19.6 g, Cholesterol 0 mg

Red Beans and Lentils

Total Time: 4 hours 15 minutes
Serves: 10

3 cups red beans, cooked
1 cup black lentils, rinsed and drained
1/4 tsp ground mustard
1/4 tsp ground nutmeg
1 tsp ground turmeric
1 tsp ground cardamom
1 1/2 tsp chili powder
3 tsp ground cumin
2 tbsp ginger, grated
6 garlic cloves, minced
5 cups water
For serving:
1 tsp garam masala
2 tsp ginger, grated
2 tsp tomato paste
1/2 cup cashew creamer
Salt

- Add all ingredients except serving ingredients into the slow cooker and stir well.
- Cover and cook on high for 4 hours.
- Add all serving ingredients and stir well.
    - Serve with rice and enjoy.

Calories 288, Fat 2.8 g, Carbohydrates 49.1 g, Sugar 2 g, Protein 18.4 g, Cholesterol 0 mg

Simple Chickpea Curry

Total Time: 6 hours 10 minutes
Serves: 6

15 oz can chickpeas
15 oz can coconut milk
15 oz can tomatoes, diced
1/4 tbsp cilantro, chopped
2 tbsp curry powder
1 tsp ginger, minced
4 garlic cloves, minced
2 onions, diced
Salt

- Add all ingredients except cilantro into the slow cooker and stir well.
- Cover and cook on low for 6 hours.
  - Garnish with cilantro and serve.

Calories 265, Fat 16.3 g, Carbohydrates 27.1 g, Sugar 4.1 g, Protein 6.4 g, Cholesterol 0 mg

Pea Chickpea Vegetable Curry

Total Time: 2 hours 15 minutes
Serves: 8

1 cup can chickpeas, drained
1 cup green peas
1 tsp red pepper flakes
1 tsp ground coriander
1 tsp ginger powder
2 tbsp curry powder
15 oz can coconut milk
2 cups vegetable broth
1 medium onion, diced
3/4 cup carrot, diced
1 1/2 cups potatoes, chopped
2 tsp sea salt

- Add all ingredients into the slow cooker and stir well.
- Cover and cook on high for 2 hours.
  - Stir well and serve.

Calories 201, Fat 12.4 g, Carbohydrates 19 g, Sugar 2.7 g, Protein 5.7 g, Cholesterol 0 mg

Perfect Curried Baked Beans

Total Time: 8 hours 10 minutes
Serves: 8

4 cups pinto beans, cooked
1 tbsp vegetable oil
1 medium onion, diced
14 oz can coconut milk
6 oz can tomato paste
2 tbsp brown sugar
1 garlic cloves, minced
1 tbsp fresh ginger, minced
3 tsp curry powder
1/8 tsp red pepper flakes
1/2 tsp cumin
1/2 tsp salt

- Add cooked beans into the slow cooker.
- Heat oil in the pan over medium heat.
- Add onion and sauté for 5 minutes.
- Add garlic and sauté for another 1 minute.
- Stir in crushed red peppers, cumin, curry powder, ginger, and salt.
- Reduce heat and stir in coconut milk, brown sugar, and tomato paste.
- Pour pan mixture over the beans and stir well.
- Cover slow cooker and cook on low for 8 hours.
- Serve and enjoy.

Calories 485, Fat 13 g, Carbohydrates 70.4 g, Sugar 7.4 g, Protein 22.9 g, Cholesterol 0 mg

Red Beans with Bell Pepper

Total Time: 5 hours 10 minutes
Serves: 4

3/4 cup celery, chopped
1 tsp dried thyme
1 tsp paprika
3/4 tsp ground red pepper
1/2 tsp ground black pepper
3 cups water
1 cup dried red beans
1 cup onion, chopped
1 cup green bell pepper, chopped
14 oz turkey sausage, sliced
1 bay leaf
5 garlic cloves, minced
1/2 tsp salt

- Add all ingredients into the slow cooker and stir well.
- Cover and cook on high for 5 hours.
  - Stir well and serve with rice.

Calories 525, Fat 29 g, Carbohydrates 35.8 g, Sugar 4.1 g, Protein 30.8 g, Cholesterol 83 mg

Spicy Black Eyed Peas

Total Time: 6 hours 30 minutes
Serves: 10

1 lb dried black-eyed peas, rinsed and drained
1 tsp ground black pepper
1 1/2 tsp cumin
1/2 tsp cayenne pepper
1 jalapeno pepper, seeded and minced
1 red bell pepper, seeded and diced
2 garlic cloves, diced
1 onion, diced
6 cups water
Salt

- Add all ingredients into the slow cooker and stir well.
- Cover and cook on low for 6 hours.
  - Serve and enjoy.

Calories 122, Fat 0.2 g, Carbohydrates 30.7 g, Sugar 2.4 g, Protein 11.4 g, Cholesterol 0 mg

Chickpea Coconut Quinoa Curry

Total Time: 4 hours 20 minutes
Serves: 8

3 cups sweet potato, peeled and cut into cubes

2 cups broccoli florets
14.5 oz can coconut milk
1/4 cup quinoa
2 garlic cloves, minced
1 tbsp ginger, grated
1 cup onion, diced
15 oz can chickpeas, drained and rinsed
28 oz can tomatoes, diced
1 tsp ground turmeric
2 tsp tamari
1 tsp chili flakes

- Add all ingredients into the slow cooker and stir well.
- Cover and cook on high for 4 hours.
  - Serve and enjoy.

Calories 291, Fat 12.2 g, Carbohydrates 41.3 g, Sugar 9.3 g, Protein 7.9 g, Cholesterol 0 mg

Red Beans Cabbage Soup

Total Time: 8 hours 10 minutes
Serves: 6

15 oz can red beans, drained and rinsed
4 cups water
4 garlic cloves, minced

1 bay leaf
1 tsp dried thyme
5 oz can tomato paste
1/2 head green cabbage, chopped
1 green bell pepper, seeded and diced
1 medium onion, diced
1 medium carrots, peeled and diced
1/4 tsp black pepper
Salt

- Add all ingredients into the slow cooker and stir well.
- Cover and cook on high for 8 hours.
  - Stir well and serve.

Calories 275, Fat 0.9 g, Carbohydrates 51.9 g, Sugar 8.6 g, Protein 18.4 g, Cholesterol 0 mg

Gluten Free Chickpea Curry

Total Time: 4 hours 10 minutes
Serves: 4

14 oz can chickpeas, drained
3 cup sweet potatoes, peeled and chopped
1/2 tsp chili flakes
1 tbsp honey
1 tsp ground cumin
2 tsp ground turmeric
2 tsp garam masala

13 oz can cream
1 tsp vegetable oil
1 tbsp fresh ginger, grated
4 garlic cloves, minced
1 large onion, chopped

- Heat oil in the pan over medium heat.
- Add onion, garlic, and ginger to the pan and sauté for 5 minutes.
- Add onion mixture into the blender along with honey, spices, cream, and salt and blend until smooth.
- Add remaining ingredients and curry blend into the slow cooker and stir well.
- Cover and cook on high for 4 hours.
    - Serve and enjoy.

Calories 636, Fat 17.9 g, Carbohydrates 113.6 g, Sugar 54.1 g, Protein 8.7 g, Cholesterol 0 mg

Vegetarian Chili Bowl

Total Time: 4 hours 20 minutes
Serves: 8

1 tsp garam masala
4 large tomatoes, peeled, seeded and chopped
1/3 cup can black beans, drained and rinsed
1/3 cup can chickpea, rinsed and drained
1 1/2 cups onions, chopped

1 cup green bell peppers, chopped
3 garlic cloves, minced
1/3 cup can red beans, rinsed and drained
1 1/2 cup vegetable stock
2 tbsp fresh cilantro, chopped
2 tbsp vegetable oil
2 green chili, minced
1/2 medium zucchini, cut into pieces
1 cup celery, chopped
1/2 tbsp chili powder
1/2 tbsp ground coriander
1/2 tsp cumin powder
1 tsp dried oregano
1 tsp dried thyme
1 tsp fresh ginger
1/4 tsp turmeric
1 1/4 tsp salt

- Heat oil in the pan over medium heat.
- Add onion, celery, green chilies, and ginger into the pan and sauté for 5 minutes.
- Add spices and stir for another 2 minutes.
- Add remaining all ingredients into the slow cooker along with pan mixture. stir well.
- Cover and cook on low for 8 hours.
    - Serve and enjoy.

Calories 135, Fat 5.7 g, Carbohydrates 19.5 g, Sugar 6.7 g, Protein 4.4 g, Cholesterol 0 mg

Healthy Turmeric Lentil Bean Chili

Total Time: 4 hours 15 minutes
Serves: 6

15 oz can red beans, rinsed and drained
1 cup coconut milk
1 tsp turmeric
1 tsp chili powder
1 tsp ground cumin
6 oz can tomato paste
2 cups water
32 oz vegetable stock
1 small onion, chopped
2 cups green lentils, rinsed and drained

- Add all ingredients except coconut milk into the slow cooker and stir well.
- Cover and cook on high for 4 hours.
- Add coconut milk and stir well.
- Stir well and serve.

Calories 598, Fat 11.5 g, Carbohydrates 92.6 g, Sugar 9.2 g, Protein 35.5 g, Cholesterol 0 mg

Chickpea Kale Sweet Potato Stew

Total Time: 4 hours 20 minutes
Serves: 8

15.5 oz can chickpeas, drained and rinsed
5 oz kale, chopped
2 red bell peppers, diced
1 1/2 lbs sweet potatoes, peeled and cut into pieces
2 tbsp curry powder
1 tsp fresh ginger, peeled and minced
3 garlic cloves, minced
2 cups vegetable broth
14.5 oz can tomatoes, drained and diced
1/4 tsp black pepper
14 oz can coconut milk
1 tsp vegetable oil
1 large onion, diced
1 tbsp kosher salt

- Heat oil in the pan over medium heat.
- Add onion and 1 tsp salt and sauté for 5 minutes.
- Add potatoes and 1 tsp salt and sauté for another 5 minutes.
- Add curry powder, garlic, and ginger and stir for 2 minutes.
- Add pan mixture into the slow cooker along with remaining ingredients except for kale and coconut milk.
- Cover and cook on high for 4 hours.
- Add coconut milk and kale and stir well. Cook for another 10 minutes.
    - Serve and enjoy.

Calories 323, Fat 12.6 g, Carbohydrates 47.7 g, Sugar 4.7 g, Protein 8 g, Cholesterol 0 mg

Chickpea Spinach Cauliflower Curry

Total Time: 6 hours 15 minutes
Serves: 6

2 cups baby spinach, chopped
15 oz can chickpeas
1/2 tbsp curry powder
1 tbsp garam masala
1 cup vegetable broth
14 oz can coconut milk
1 sweet potato, peeled and diced
2 cups cauliflower florets
2 cups can tomatoes, chopped
1 tbsp ginger, minced
1 garlic clove, minced
1/2 onion, chopped
1 tsp vegetable oil
1 tsp salt

- Heat oil in the pan over medium heat.
- Add ginger, garlic, and onion to the pan and sauté for 5 minutes.
- Add pan mixture into the slow cooker with remaining ingredients except for spinach.
- Cover and cook on low for 6 hours.
- Add spinach and stir well.

- Serve with rice and enjoy.

Calories 282, Fat 16.1 g, Carbohydrates 30.1 g, Sugar 5.3 g, Protein 8 g, Cholesterol 0 mg

Spicy Winter Chickpeas

Total Time: 6 hours 15 minutes
Serves: 4

1 1/2 cups dried chickpeas, rinsed and drained
2 tbsp parsley, chopped
1 tbsp lemon juice
1 bay leaf
1/2 butternut squash, cut into 1-inch cubes
10 green olive, pitted
1 tsp tamarind paste
2 garlic cloves, minced
2 tomatoes, diced
1 large onion, chopped
2 tbsp vegetable oil
1/2 tsp ground black pepper
1 tsp curry powder
1 tsp ground ginger
1 tsp garam masala
1 tsp smoked paprika
1 tsp turmeric
1/2 tsp salt

- Heat oil in the pan over medium heat.
- Add garlic, ginger, and onion to the pan and sauté for 5 minutes.
- Add spices and sauté for 1 minute. Transfer mixture into the slow cooker.

- Add remaining ingredients into the slow cooker and stir well.
- Cover and cook on low for 6 hours.
  - Serve and enjoy.

Calories 425, Fat 14.3 g, Carbohydrates 60.5 g, Sugar 12.6 g, Protein 16.3 g, Cholesterol 0 mg

Spicy Curried Chickpeas

Total Time: 6 hours 20 minutes
Serves: 4

1.1 lbs chickpeas, rinsed and drained
1/2 tsp dried herbs
1/2 tsp nutmeg
1/2 tsp garam masala
1/2 tsp coriander powder
1 tsp tomato puree
14 oz tomatoes, chopped
2 garlic cloves, minced
2 onion, chopped
1 tsp cumin seeds
4 tsp vegetable oil
2 bay leaves
Salt

- Soaked chickpeas in a water for overnight.
- Heat oil in the pan over medium heat.
- Add cumin seeds, garlic, and onion into the pan and sauté for 5 minutes.
- Add tomato paste, tomatoes and spices and sauté for 2 minutes. Transfer pan mixture into the blender and blend until smooth.
- Add chickpeas, bay leaves, and blended puree into the slow cooker and stir well.
- Cover and cook on low for 6 hours.

- Serve with rice and enjoy.

Calories 540, Fat 12.6 g, Carbohydrates 85.7 g, Sugar 18.5 g, Protein 25.8 g, Cholesterol 0 mg

Spiced Green Peas Rice

Total Time: 2 hours 20 minutes
Serves: 6

1 cup green peas
2 tsp chili powder
2 tomatoes, pureed
1 tsp turmeric powder
2 green chilies, chopped
1 tsp cumin seeds
1 tbsp vegetable oil
2 potatoes, peeled and chopped
1 cup basmati rice, rinsed and drained
2 cups water

- Add water, rice, and potatoes into the slow cooker.
- Heat oil in the pan over medium heat.
- Add cumin seeds, turmeric, chili powder, tomato puree, green chilies, and salt to the pan and sauté for 2 minutes.
- Transfer pan mixture into the slow cooker and stir well.
- Cover and cook on high for 1 1/2 hours.
- Add green peas and cook for another 30 minutes.
- Serve and enjoy.

Calories 214, Fat 3 g, Carbohydrates 41.8 g, Sugar 3.4 g, Protein 5.3 g, Cholesterol 0 mg

Buttered Peas Rice

Total Time: 2 hours 15 minutes
Serves: 4

1 cup brown rice, uncooked
2 tbsp green onion, sliced
1 cup frozen peas
1 bell pepper, chopped
2 tbsp butter
1 1/4 cup water
Pepper
Salt

- Add all ingredients into the slow cooker and mix well.
- Cover and cook on high for 2 hours.
    - Serve and enjoy.

Calories 265, Fat 7.2 g, Carbohydrates 44.4 g, Sugar 3.4 g, Protein 6 g, Cholesterol 15 mg

VEGETABLE RECIPES

Delicious Spiced Potatoes and Cauliflower

Total Time: 4 hours 15 minutes
Serves: 8

1 large cauliflower head, cut into florets
1 large potato, peeled and diced
1 tsp fresh ginger, grated
2 cloves garlic, minced
2 jalapeno peppers, sliced
1 medium onion, peeled and diced
1 medium tomato, diced
1 tbsp cumin seeds
1 tsp turmeric
3 tbsp vegetable oil
1 tbsp fresh cilantro, chopped
1/4 tsp cayenne pepper
1 tbsp garam masala
1 tbsp kosher salt

- Add all ingredients except cilantro into the slow cooker and mix well.
- Cover and cook on low for 4 hours.
  - Garnish with cilantro and serve.

Calories 123, Fat 5.6 g, Carbohydrates 16.7 g, Sugar 4 g, Protein 3.6 g, Cholesterol 0 mg

Scrumptious Spinach Paneer

Total Time: 5 hours 15 minutes
Serves: 6

12 oz paneer cheese
8 oz fresh spinach, chopped
30 oz frozen spinach, thawed
14 oz can coconut milk
1/8 tsp cayenne pepper
1 tbsp ground cumin
1 tbsp ground coriander
1 tbsp garam masala
1 1/2 cups can tomato sauce
3 tbsp fresh ginger, minced
4 garlic cloves, chopped
1 tsp salt

- Add all ingredients except fresh spinach and paneer into the slow cooker.
- Cover and cook on low for 3 hours.

- Add fresh spinach and cook for 1 hour.
- Using immersion blender blend mixture until smooth.
- Add paneer cheese and cook for 1 hour.

- Serve and enjoy.

Calories 220, Fat 10 g, Carbohydrates 16 g, Sugar 6 g, Protein 20 g, Cholesterol 0 mg

Tasty Spinach Potato

Total Time: 3 hours 15 minutes
Serves: 4

1 1/2 lbs potatoes, peel and cut into chunks
1/2 lb fresh spinach, chopped
1/2 tsp chili powder
1/2 tsp garam masala
1/2 tsp ground coriander
1/2 tsp cumin
1 tbsp vegetable oil
1/4 cup water
1/2 onion, sliced
Pepper
Salt

- Add all ingredients into the slow cooker and stir well.
- Cover and cook on low for 3 hours.
  - Serve and enjoy.

Calories 168, Fat 3.9 g, Carbohydrates 30.4 g, Sugar 2.8 g, Protein 4.7 g, Cholesterol 0 mg

Spicy Eggplant Potatoes

Total Time: 2 hours 40 minutes
Serves: 8

2 medium eggplants, cut into 1-inch cubes
1 large potato, peeled and cut into 1/2 inch cubes
2 jalapeño chilies, seeded and minced
1 tbsp ground cumin
1 tbsp chili powder
1 medium onion, chopped
1 tsp ginger, grated
6 garlic cloves, minced
1 tbsp garam masala
1 tsp turmeric
2 tbsp fresh cilantro, chopped
1/4 cup vegetable oil
1 tbsp kosher salt

- Add all ingredients into the slow cooker and stir well.
- Cover and cook on high for 2 hours.
- Remove lid and cook on low for another 30 minutes.
- Serve and enjoy.

Calories 147, Fat 7.5 g, Carbohydrates 19.4 g, Sugar 5.2 g, Protein 2.9 g, Cholesterol 0 mg

Healthy Vegetable Coconut Curry

Total Time: 4 hours 20 minutes
Serves: 8

1/4 cup cilantro, chopped
1 cup green peas
1 1/2 cups carrots, peeled and cut into strips
14 oz can coconut milk
1 oz dry onion soup mix
2 bell pepper, cut into strips
1/2 tsp cayenne pepper
1/2 tsp red pepper flakes
1 tbsp chili powder
2 tbsp flour
1/4 cup curry powder
5 potatoes, peeled and cut into cubes
Water as needed

- Add all ingredients into the slow cooker and mix well.
- Cover and cook on low for 4 hours.
  - Stir well and serve.

Calories 370, Fat 18.3 g, Carbohydrates 48.8 g, Sugar 5.4 g, Protein 8.2 g, Cholesterol 0 mg

Easy Whole Cauliflower Curry

Total Time: 4 hours 15 minutes
Serves: 4

1 large cauliflower head, trimmed
2 garlic cloves, sliced
1/2 onion, chopped
2 small potatoes, quartered
1 red pepper, sliced
For sauce:
1/2 tsp cayenne pepper
1 tsp cumin
2 tbsp curry powder
2 cups can coconut milk
2 cups vegetable broth

- Add red pepper, potatoes, onion, garlic, and cauliflower into the slow cooker.
- In a bowl, whisk together all sauce ingredients and pour over cauliflower.
- Cover and cook on low for 4 hours.
- About 15 minutes before serving add coconut milk and stir well.
- Serve and enjoy.

Calories 383, Fat 25.8 g, Carbohydrates 34.3 g, Sugar 8.6 g, Protein 11.4 g, Cholesterol 0 mg

Vegetable Curried Rice

Total Time: 4 hours 10 minutes
Serves: 4

1 1/2 cups green cabbage, chopped
2 cups mushrooms, chopped
1 cup broccoli, chopped
1 cup brown rice
1 tsp curry powder
2 tbsp apple cider vinegar
1/4 tsp dried thyme
1/2 tsp garlic powder
1/2 tsp black pepper
4 cups vegetable broth
1 tsp salt

- Add all ingredients into the slow cooker and mix well.
- Cover and cook on low for 4 hours.
- Using fork fluff the rice.
- Serve and enjoy.

Calories 237, Fat 2.9 g, Carbohydrates 42.1 g, Sugar 2.7 g, Protein 10.7 g, Cholesterol 0 mg

Curried Zucchini Eggplant

Total Time: 4 hours 15 minutes
Serves: 4

4 cups zucchini, chopped
4 cups eggplant, peeled and chopped
1/4 cup vegetable broth
15 oz can coconut milk
6 oz can tomato paste
1/4 tsp cumin
1/4 tsp cayenne pepper
1 tbsp garam masala
1 tbsp curry powder
4 garlic cloves, minced
1 onion, chopped
1 tsp salt

- Add all ingredients into the slow cooker and mix well.
- Cover and cook on low for 4 hours.
  - Stir well and serve with rice.

Calories 307, Fat 23.6 g, Carbohydrates 24.3 g, Sugar 10.9 g, Protein 7.2 g, Cholesterol 0 mg

Flavourful Vegetable Korma

Total Time: 5 hours 15 minutes
Serves: 4

2 tbsp almond meal
1 tbsp red pepper flakes
1 tsp garam masala
2 tbsp curry powder
10 oz coconut milk
2 garlic cloves, minced
1/2 large onion, chopped
1 cup green beans, chopped
1/2 cup frozen green peas
2 large carrots, chopped
1 large cauliflower head, cut into florets
1 tsp sea salt

- Add all ingredients into the slow cooker and stir well.
- Cover and cook on high for 5 hours.
  - Serve and enjoy.

Calories 295, Fat 19.4 g, Carbohydrates 28.7 g, Sugar 11.8 g, Protein 9.1 g, Cholesterol 0 mg

Potato Okra Curry

Total Time: 3 hours 15 minutes
Serves: 6

1 1/2 lbs potatoes, peeled and cut into pieces
1 lb okra, cut the ends and sliced
2 cups vegetable stock
13 oz can coconut milk
1 1/2 tbsp curry powder
3/4 tsp red pepper flakes
2 tsp fresh ginger, grated
4 garlic cloves, minced
1 large onion, chopped
1 1/2 tbsp vegetable oil
1 bell pepper, seeded and chopped
1 1/2 tsp salt

- Add potatoes, bell pepper, and okra into the slow cooker.
- Heat oil in a pan over medium heat.
- Add garlic, onion, and ginger to the pan and sauté for 5 minutes.
- Remove pan from heat and stir in spices.
- Transfer pan mixture into the slow cooker and stir well.
- Cover and cook on low for 3 hours.
- Stir well and serve with rice.

Calories 290, Fat 17.8 g, Carbohydrates 31.8 g, Sugar 5.3 g, Protein 5.5 g, Cholesterol 0 mg

Delicious Navratan Korma

Total Time: 8 hours 15 minutes
Serves: 4

1 cup cauliflower florets
1/2 cup tomatoes, diced
1/2 cup green peas
1 cup carrots, chopped
2 tbsp sour cream
1/4 cup coconut milk
1 tbsp raisins
1/4 tsp chili powder
1/2 tsp ground coriander
1/2 tsp ground turmeric
1 tbsp ginger, grated
2 tbsp bell pepper, minced
1/4 onion, chopped
1/2 cup water
Salt

- Add all ingredients except sour cream into the slow cooker and stir well.
- Cover and cook on low for 8 hours.
  - Stir in sour cream and serve with rice.

Calories 118, Fat 5.3 g, Carbohydrates 16.8 g, Sugar 8.8 g, Protein 3.4 g, Cholesterol 3 mg

Slow Cooker Sambar

Total Time: 6 hours 10 minutes
Serves: 2

1/4 cup pink lentils
1 cup water
1/2 tsp tamarind paste
1 tsp sambar powder
4 curry leaves
1/4 cup tomatoes, chopped
1/4 cup eggplants, cut into pieces
1/4 cup pumpkin, cut into pieces
1 medium onion, sliced
1 drumstick, peeled and cut into pieces
Salt

- Add all ingredients into the slow cooker and stir well.
- Cover and cook on low for 6 hours.
  - Stir well and serve hot with rice.

Calories 130, Fat 0.6 g, Carbohydrates 24.7 g, Sugar 5.3 g, Protein 7.5 g, Cholesterol 0 mg

Creamy Carrot Squash Soup

Total Time: 6 hours 15 minutes
Serves: 8

1 lb butternut squash, peeled and diced
1/2 lb carrots, peeled and cut into chunks
13.5 oz can coconut milk
1/4 tsp ground sage
1 tsp pepper
1 bay leaf
3 cups vegetable broth
1 apple, peeled and sliced
1 medium onion, diced
1 tsp salt

- Add squash, bay leaf, apple, carrots, onion, and broth into the slow cooker.
- Cover and cook on low for 6 hours.
- Discard bay leaf and using immersion blender blend until smooth.
- Add coconut milk, sage, pepper, and salt. Stir well.
- Serve and enjoy.

Calories 163, Fat 11.3 g, Carbohydrates 15.8 g, Sugar 5.1 g, Protein 3.8 g, Cholesterol 0 mg

Yummy Slow Cooked Potatoes

Total Time: 6 hours 15 minutes
Serves: 4

2.2 lbs potatoes, peel and cut into cubes
1/2 tsp chili powder
1/2 tsp cumin
1 1/2 tsp turmeric
1 tsp garam masala
1 tsp ground ginger
1 tsp mustard seeds
4 tomatoes, chopped
1/4 tsp red chili flakes
1 tbsp vegetable oil
1 tsp salt

- In a bowl, mix together chili flakes, chili powder, cumin, turmeric, garam masala, and ginger.
- Heat oil in the pan over medium heat.
- Add mustard seeds into the pan and stir until they start to pop then add onion and sauté until lightly brown.
- Add mixed spices and stir for a minute.
- Add tomatoes and salt and stir for a minute.
- Place potatoes in the slow cooker then pour pan mixture over the potatoes.
- Cover and cook on low for 6 hours.
    - Stir well and serve.

Calories 235, Fat 4.4 g, Carbohydrates 45.8 g, Sugar 6.2 g, Protein 5.7 g, Cholesterol 0 mg

Curried Potatoes

Total Time: 6 hours 15 minutes
Serves: 6

7 potatoes, washed and cut into chunks
2 tsp sugar
2 tsp chili powder
2 tsp curry powder
2 tsp paprika
14.5 oz can tomatoes, diced
1 tbsp vegetable oil
1/2 tsp kosher salt

- Add all ingredients into the slow cooker and stir well.
- Cover and cook on low for 6 hours.
    - Serve and enjoy.

Calories 218, Fat 2.9 g, Carbohydrates 45.1 g, Sugar 6.7 g, Protein 5.1 g, Cholesterol 0 mg

Mushroom Eggplant Potato Curry

Total Time: 4 hours 15 minutes
Serves: 6

8 mushrooms, quartered
1 large eggplant, peeled and cut into 1-inch pieces
3 potatoes, peeled and cut into 1/2 inch cubes
1 bay leaf
2 tsp fresh ginger, grated
14 oz can tomatoes, chopped
1/2 cup red pepper, chopped
1 tsp black pepper
1 tbsp ground cumin
2 garlic cloves, minced
1 large onion, chopped
2 tbsp vegetable oil
1 tsp lime juice
Salt

- Heat oil in the pan over medium heat.
- Add eggplant to the pan and sauté until lightly brown.
- Transfer eggplant to the slow cooker.
- In the same pan, add onion and sauté for 3 minutes. Add garlic, pepper, and cumin and sauté for a minute.
- Transfer onion mixture to the slow cooker along with remaining all ingredients and stir well.
- Cover and cook on high for 4 hours.
    - Stir well and serve.

Calories 173, Fat 5.3 g, Carbohydrates 29.4 g, Sugar 6.7 g, Protein 4.6 g, Cholesterol 0 mg

Eggplant Chickpea Curry

Total Time: 8 hours 40 minutes
Serves: 6

15 oz can chickpeas, rinsed and drained
1 tbsp fresh ginger, minced
2 tsp cumin
1 tbsp garam masala
1 tbsp curry powder
3 cups vegetable broth
15 oz can tomatoes
4 garlic cloves, minced
3 lbs eggplant, diced
2 cups onion, diced
2 tsp salt

- Add all ingredients except chickpeas into the slow cooker.
- Cover and cook on low for 8 hours.
- Add chickpeas and cook for another 30 minutes.
- Stir well and serve.

Calories 203, Fat 2.3 g, Carbohydrates 39.2 g, Sugar 11.3 g, Protein 9.7 g, Cholesterol 0 mg

Coconut Eggplant Curry

Total Time: 4 hours 10 minutes
Serves: 6

2 lbs eggplant, cut into 1 inch cubed
4 garlic cloves, minced
14.5 oz can coconut milk
6 oz tomato paste
1 tbsp curry powder
1 medium onion, chopped
1 green bell pepper, seeded and chopped
2 Serrano peppers, seeded and minced
1 tbsp garam masala
1 tsp salt

- Add all ingredients into the slow cooker and stir well.
- Cover and cook on low for 4 hours.
    - Serve and enjoy.

Calories 216, Fat 15.2 g, Carbohydrates 20.7 g, Sugar 9.8 g, Protein 4.8 g, Cholesterol 0 mg

Creamy Cauliflower Soup

Total Time: 4 hours 20 minutes
Serves: 6

1 cauliflower head
2 cups vegetable broth
3 garlic cloves
1/4 cup dried cranberries
1/4 cup pine nuts
13.5 oz can coconut milk
5.3 oz plain yogurt
1 tbsp curry powder
1 tbsp water
3/4 tsp garam masala
1/2 cup sugar
1/2 tsp salt

- Add cauliflower, broth, and garlic into the slow cooker. Cover and cook on low for 4 hours.
- Add cauliflower mixture into the blender along with yogurt and coconut milk and blend until smooth.
- Pour into the six serving bowls.
- In a pan, cook over medium heat pine nuts with water, garam masala, and sugar. Cook until sugar is crystallized.
- Sprinkle pan mixture over the soup.
    - Serve and enjoy.

Calories 276, Fat 18.5 g, Carbohydrates 25.1 g, Sugar 20.1 g, Protein 6.2 g, Cholesterol 2 mg

Delicious Sweet Potato Curry

Total Time: 6 hours 15 minutes
Serves: 6

1 sweet potato, diced
1 courgette, diced
1/4 cup cashew nuts
14 oz can tomatoes, chopped
1 tsp curry powder
1/2 tsp chili powder
1/2 tsp black pepper
2 tbsp tomato puree
4 tbsp flour
14 oz can coconut milk
1 tsp garlic, minced
2 onions, diced
4 tomatoes, diced
1 tsp ginger, minced
2 tsp garam masala
1 tbsp vegetable oil

- Heat oil in the pan over medium heat.
- Add ginger, onion, and garlic to the pan and sauté for 5 minutes.
- Add tomato paste, flour, and spices and cook for a minute.
- Add coconut milk and stir well and cook until thickened.

- Transfer pan mixture into the slow cooker along with remaining ingredients and mix well.
- Cover and cook on low for 6 hours.
  - Serve and enjoy.

Calories 275, Fat 19.5 g, Carbohydrates 24 g, Sugar 8.3 g, Protein 5.5 g, Cholesterol 0 mg

Flavorful Vegetable Curry

Total Time: 7 hours 15 minutes
Serves: 4

15 oz can chickpeas, rinsed and drained
8 oz fresh green beans, cut into 1-inch pieces
4 medium carrots, sliced
2 medium potatoes, cut into 1/2 inch cubes
1 cup onion, chopped
14 oz can vegetable broth
14 oz can tomatoes, diced
2 tbsp tapioca
2 tsp curry powder
1 tsp ground coriander
3 garlic cloves, minced
1/8 tsp ground cinnamon
1/4 tsp red pepper, crushed
1/4 tsp salt

- Add all ingredients into the slow cooker and stir well.

- Cover and cook on low for 7 hours.

  - Stir well and serve with rice.

Calories 367, Fat 3.1 g, Carbohydrates 75.3 g Sugar 11.8 g, Protein 12.6 g, Cholesterol 1 mg

Delicious Tofu Coconut Curry

Total Time: 4 hours 15 minutes
Serves: 4

1 cup firm tofu, diced
2 tsp garlic cloves, minced
1 cup onion, chopped
8 oz tomato paste
2 cups bell pepper, chopped
1 tbsp garam masala
2 tbsp butter
1 tbsp curry powder
10 oz can coconut milk
1 1/2 tsp sea salt

- Add all ingredients into the slow cooker and stir well.
- Cover and cook on low for 4 hours.
  - Stir well and serve with rice.

Calories 179, Fat 9.1 g, Carbohydrates 20.4 g, Sugar 11.6 g, Protein 8.9 g, Cholesterol 15 mg

Creamy Coconut Pumpkin Curry

Total Time: 6 hours 15 minutes
Serves: 6

15 oz can coconut milk, unsweetened
2 cups pumpkin puree
1 cup vegetable stock
3 carrots, cut into 1-inch pieces
3 cups sweet potatoes, cut into 1-inch cubes
1/2 tbsp curry powder
1/4 tsp turmeric powder
1/4 tsp ground black pepper
1/2 large onion, diced
1 garlic clove, minced
2 chicken breasts, cut into 1-inch cubes
1 lime juice
2 tsp garam masala
1/2 tsp kosher salt

- Add all ingredients into the slow cooker and mix well.
- Cover and cook on low for 6 hours.
  - Serve with rice and enjoy.

Calories 357, Fat 17.7 g, Carbohydrates 35 g, Sugar 7.4 g, Protein 17.6 g, Cholesterol 43 mg

Hearty Potato Curry

Total Time: 8 hours 10 minutes
Serves: 4

1 lb potatoes, cut into 1-inch cubes
1/2 tsp cumin
1/2 tsp coriander
1/2 tsp peppercorns
1 cinnamon stick
1 cups vegetable stock
1 tsp tamarind paste
1 bay leaf
1/4 tsp red pepper, crushed
1/2 tsp garam masala
4 garlic cloves, minced
2 tsp ginger, minced
1 onion, diced
2 tbsp vegetable oil
1 1/2 tsp paprika
1 1/2 tsp turmeric
1/2 cup frozen peas
2 cups coconut milk
2 tbsp all purpose flour
Pepper
Salt

- Heat 1 tbsp oil in the pan over medium heat.
- Add onion and cook until golden brown, about 3 minutes.

- Add powder spices and stir for 1 minute.
- Transfer onion mixture to the blender with tamarind, ginger, garlic, and coconut milk and blend until smooth.
- Pour blended mixture into the slow cooker with remaining ingredients except for peas and flour.
- Cover and cook on low for 8 hours.
- Add peas and stir well. Whisk flour in little water and pour into the slow cooker.
  - Stir well and serve.

Calories 476, Fat 36.5 g, Carbohydrates 37.2 g, Sugar 8.8 g, Protein 7 g, Cholesterol 0 mg

Mix Vegetable Curry

Total Time: 6 hours 10 minutes
Serves: 4

3 1/2 cups broccoli florets
2.5 oz green beans
2 medium carrots, peeled and sliced
2 large sweet potatoes, diced
3 tbsp tomato puree
14 oz can coconut milk
1 red chili, seeded and chopped
1 tsp garam masala
1 tsp ground turmeric
2 tsp ground coriander
2 tsp ground cumin
1 tsp chili powder
1 tsp ginger, grated
1 tsp garlic, grated
1 onion, diced

- Add all ingredients except green beans into the slow cooker and mix well.
- Cover and cook on low for 5 hours.
- Add green beans and stir well and cook for another 1 hour.
  - Serve with rice.

Calories 313, Fat 22 g, Carbohydrates 28.3 g, Sugar 5.1 g, Protein 6.3 g, Cholesterol 0 mg

MEAT RECIPES

Tasty Chicken Tikka Masala

Total Time: 6 hours 25 minutes
Serves: 6

2 lbs chicken thighs, skinless and boneless, cut into 2-inch pieces
10 oz frozen peas, thawed
1 1/2 cups heavy cream
1 tbsp cornstarch
1 tbsp sugar
28 oz can tomatoes
1 tsp ginger, grated
3 tbsp garam masala
1/2 tsp red pepper flakes
6 garlic cloves, minced
1 large onion, diced
2 tbsp vegetable oil
1 cup plain yogurt
1 tbsp ground cumin
1 tbsp ground coriander
1 tsp kosher salt

- In a large bowl, combine together chicken, yogurt, cumin, ground coriander, and salt. Marinade for 10 minutes.
- Heat 1 tbsp oil in the pan over medium-high heat.
- Place marinated chicken into the pan and cook until lightly brown on both the sides.
- Transfer chicken into the slow cooker.
- In the same pan, heat remaining oil. Add onions, red pepper flakes, and garlic and saute for 5 minutes.
- Add ginger, garam masala, and salt and cook for 1 minute.
- Add sugar and tomatoes, turn heat to high and bring to boil. Transfer into the slow cooker.
- Cover and cook on low for 6 hours.
- Whisk together 1/4 cup heavy cream and cornstarch and add to the slow cooker along with remaining peas and heavy cream.
- Stir to mix and cover and cook for another 10 minutes.
  - Serve and enjoy.

Calories 557, Fat 27.8 g, Carbohydrates 24.5 g, Sugar 12.7 g, Protein 51.1 g, Cholesterol 178 mg

Delicious Chicken Tandoori

Total Time: 8 hours 20 minutes
Serves: 4

14 oz coconut milk
4 chicken thighs
1 tsp fresh ginger, grated
1 tsp paprika
1 tsp cayenne pepper
2 tsp tomato paste
2 tsp garam masala
1 tsp ground coriander
1 tsp ground cumin

- Add all ingredients into the slow cooker and mix well.
- Cover and cook on low for 8 hours.
    - Serve and enjoy.

Calories 514, Fat 34.8 g, Carbohydrates 7.1 g, Sugar 3.8 g, Protein 44.9 g, Cholesterol 130 mg

Peanut Butter Chicken

Total Time: 4 hours 30 minutes
Serves: 6

3 chicken breasts, skinless and boneless
1 tbsp lime juice
2 tbsp cornstarch
3 garlic cloves, minced
1 tbsp ginger, minced
1 tbsp rice wine vinegar
2 tbsp honey
2 tbsp soy sauce
1/3 cup creamy peanut butter
1 cup coconut milk

- Add all ingredients except lime juice and cornstarch into the slow cooker and mix well.
- Cover and cook on low for 4 hours.
- Whisk together cornstarch and 2 tbsp water and pour into the slow cooker.
- Stir well and cook for another 20 minutes until gravy thickens.
- Serve and enjoy.

Calories 356, Fat 22.2 g, Carbohydrates 15.4 g, Sugar 8.7 g, Protein 26.2 g, Cholesterol 65 mg

Spicy Chicken Curry

Total Time: 6 hours 20 minutes
Serves: 4

4 chicken thighs, boneless and cut into chunks
3 tbsp flour
2 tsp ground coriander
2 tsp garam masala
2 tsp turmeric
2 tsp ground cumin
1 tsp ginger, grated
1/2 lemon juice
4 garlic cloves, crushed
2 onion, chopped
2 green chilies, chopped
14 oz can tomatoes, chopped
1 tbsp vegetable oil

- Add ginger, chilies, garlic, and onion into the blender and blend until smooth.
- Heat oil in the pan over medium heat.
- Add blended puree into the pan and sauté for 3 minutes.
- Add spices and sauté for 2-3 minutes.
- Add flour and tomatoes into the pan and stir well.
- Refill tomato can halfway with water and adds in the pan. Stir well.
- Add chicken into the slow cooker and season with pepper and salt.

- Pour pan mixture over the chicken with lemon juice.
- Cover and cook on low for 6 hours.
  - Serve and enjoy.

Calories 387, Fat 14.8 g, Carbohydrates 17.3 g, Sugar 6 g, Protein 44.9 g, Cholesterol 130 mg

Juicy and Tender Goat Curry

Total Time: 5 hours 15 minutes
Serves: 6

2 lbs goat meat
2 Serrano pepper, minced
1 tsp paprika
1 tsp chili powder
1 tsp turmeric powder
1 tsp cumin powder
1 tbsp coriander powder
2 cardamom pods
2 garlic cloves, minced
1 tbsp ghee
1 bay leaf
3 whole cloves
1 tsp fresh ginger, minced
1 large onion, chopped
1 cup water
1 tsp garam masala
28 oz can tomatoes, diced
2 tsp salt

- Add cardamom and cloves into the grinder and grind well.
- Add all ingredients into the slow cooker except water, garam masala, and tomatoes.
- Cover and cook on high for 4 hours.
- Add water, garam masala, and tomatoes and stir well.
- Cook for another 1 hour until meat is tender.
    - Serve and enjoy.

Calories 230, **Fat** 5.9 g, **Carbohydrates** 10.6 g, **Sugar** 5.8 g, **Protein** 33.6 g, **Cholesterol** 92 mg

Delicious Slow Cooked Beef

Total Time: 6 hours 15 minutes
Serves: 4

2 lbs beef chuck steak, diced
1/2 cup coriander, chopped
2 cardamom pods
1 cinnamon stick
14 oz can tomatoes, diced
1/4 cup curry paste
1 red chili, chopped
1 tsp ginger, grated
2 garlic cloves, crushed
1 large onion, sliced
2 tbsp vegetable oil
1/4 cup plain flour

- Add beef and flour into the ziplock bag and shake well.
- Heat oil in the saucepan over medium heat.
- Add beef into the saucepan and cook for 3-4 minutes or until lightly brown. Transfer beef into the slow cooker.
- In the same pan, add onion, ginger, and garlic and sauté for 4 minutes.
- Add curry paste and chili and stir for 1 minute.

- Add 3/4 cup water, tomatoes, cardamom, and cinnamon and stir well. Transfer mixture into the slow cooker.
- Cover and cook on low for 5 1/2 hours or until beef is tender.
- Add coriander and stir well.

- Serve and enjoy.

Calories 651, Fat 29.9 g, Carbohydrates 19.7 g, Sugar 5 g, Protein 71.8 g, Cholesterol 203 mg

Simple Beef Curry

Total Time: 8 hours 40 minutes
Serves: 4

12 oz beef steak, cut into 1-inch pieces
2 onions, chopped
14 oz can tomatoes, chopped
2 tsp garam masala
4 garlic cloves, chopped
4 tsp ground cumin
4 tsp ground coriander
2 tsp ground turmeric
2 chilies, chopped
1 tsp ginger, grated
7 oz yogurt
4 tbsp vegetable oil

- Heat oil in the pan over medium heat.
- Add beef to the pan and cook for 4-5 minutes or until lightly brown. Transfer beef into the slow cooker.
- In the same pan, sauté onion, ginger, chili, and garlic for 2 minutes.
- Add spices and stir-fry for 1 minute. Transfer pan mixture to the slow cooker.
- Add remaining ingredients except for yogurt into the slow cooker and stir well.
- Cover and cook on low for 8 hours.
- Add yogurt and stir well and cook for another 30 minutes.
  - Serve and enjoy.

Calories 375, Fat 20.2 g, Carbohydrates 16.7 g, Sugar 9.3 g, Protein 30.8 g, Cholesterol 79 mg

Easy Curried Chicken

Total Time: 4 hours 15 minutes
Serves: 4

2 tbsp tomato paste
14 oz can coconut milk
3 garlic cloves, minced
2 tbsp fresh ginger, minced
1 tsp cumin
1 tsp turmeric
1 tsp garam masala
1 cinnamon stick
2 bay leaves
1 1/2 lbs chicken thighs
1 medium onion, diced
1/4 cup fresh cilantro, chopped
1 1/2 tsp salt

- Add all ingredients into the slow cooker and stir well.
- Cover and cook on low for 4 hours.
- Using fork shred the meat and stir well into the sauce.
- Serve and enjoy.

Calories 553, Fat 34.2 g, Carbohydrates 10.2 g, Sugar 2.3 g, Protein 52.4 g, Cholesterol 151 mg

Chicken Vegetable Curry

Total Time: 3 hours 25 minutes
Serves: 4

2 cups mushrooms, sliced
1 cup green peas
3 chicken breasts, skinless, boneless and cut into pieces
2 tsp ground cayenne
1/2 tsp black pepper
3 tbsp curry powder
1 packet dry onion soup mix
14 oz can coconut milk
10.75 oz can chicken soup
10.75 oz can mushroom soup
1 onion, chopped
1 tbsp butter

- Melt butter in the pan over medium heat.
- Add onion and cook for 5 minutes. Transfer to the slow cooker.
- Add remaining ingredients and stir well.
- Cover and cook on high for 1 1/2 hours then reduce heat to low and cook for another 1 1/2 hours.
- Serve and enjoy.

Calories 635, Fat 37.9 g, Carbohydrates 32 g, Sugar 2.3 g, Protein 45.2 g, Cholesterol 111 mg

Spicy Cauliflower Chicken

Total Time: 6 hours 15 minutes
Serves: 4

1 1/2 lbs chicken thighs, skinless, boneless and cut into halves
1 small cauliflower head, cut into florets
1/4 cup raisins
1 onion, chopped
1 tbsp curry powder
2 tbsp ginger, grated
2 tbsp tomato paste
28 oz can tomatoes, diced
1/2 tsp kosher salt

- Add all ingredients into the slow cooker and stir well.
- Cover and cook on low for 6 hours.
  - Serve and enjoy.

Calories 391, Fat 17.3 g, Carbohydrates 26.7 g, Sugar 6.7 g, Protein 31.1 g, Cholesterol 96 mg

Yummy Butter Chicken

Total Time: 4 hours 30 minutes
Serves: 6

4 large chicken thighs, skinless, boneless and cut into pieces
14 oz can coconut milk
1 cup plain yogurt
15 green cardamom pods
6 oz can tomato paste
1 tsp garam masala
2 tsp tandoori masala
1 tsp curry paste
2 tsp curry powder
3 garlic cloves, minced
1 onion, diced
3 tbsp vegetable oil
2 tbsp butter
Salt

- Heat butter and oil in a pan over medium heat.
- Add chicken, garlic, and onion to the pan and cook until onion softens.
- Stir in tomato paste, garam masala, tandoori masala, curry paste, and curry powder.
- Transfer chicken mixture into the slow cooker.
- Stir in yogurt, coconut milk, and cardamom pods.
- Season with salt.
- Cover and cook on high for 4 hours.

- Serve and enjoy.

Calories 480, Fat 33.3 g, Carbohydrates 17.2 g, Sugar 7.1 g, Protein 30.6 g, Cholesterol 103 mg

Lamb Curry

Total Time: 8 hours 15 minutes
Serves: 6

2 lbs lamb meat, cut into 1 1/2" cubes
1/4 cup cilantro, chopped
20 almonds
1/4 tsp saffron threads
1 cup plain yogurt
1/2 tsp turmeric
2 large onion, sliced
6 tbsp vegetable oil
3 tomatoes, chopped
1/4 cup dried coconut, unsweetened
5 garlic cloves, crushed
1 tsp fresh ginger, grated
1 tsp garam masala
1 tsp cumin seeds
3 green Chile pepper
4 dried red Chile pepper
Salt

- Add tomatoes, grated coconut, garlic, ginger, garam masala, cumin seeds, green chilies, and red chilies into the blender and blend until smooth.
- Heat oil in a pan over medium heat.
- Add onion to the pan and sauté for 5 minutes or until softened.

- Add spice paste to the pan and cook for 3 minutes.
- Stir in meat and salt. Cook over medium heat for 8 minutes.
- Mix in almonds, saffron, and yogurt until well combined.
- Transfer pan mixture into the slow cooker and stir well.
- Cover and cook on low for 8 hours.
    - Serve and enjoy.

Calories 489, Fat 35.4 g, Carbohydrates 16.1 g, Sugar 7.1 g, Protein 28.1 g, Cholesterol 88 mg

Chicken Quinoa Curry

Total Time: 4 hours 45 minutes
Serves: 6

1 1/2 lbs chicken breast, diced
1/3 cup quinoa
1/4 tsp paprika
1 tbsp curry powder
1/4 cup coconut milk
1 cup chicken broth
1 3/4 cups apples, chopped
1 1/4 cups celery, chopped
3/4 cup onion, chopped

- Add all ingredients except quinoa into the slow cooker and stir well.
- Cover and cook on low for 4 hours.
- Add quinoa and stir well. Cook for another 35 minutes.
- Stir well and serve.

Calories 185, Fat 3.1 g, Carbohydrates 14.4 g, Sugar 8.2 g, Protein 24.4 g, Cholesterol 59 mg

Delicious Chicken Stew

Total Time: 4 hours 15 minutes
Serves: 8

2 lbs chicken thighs, skinless, boneless and cut into pieces
1 medium onion, chopped
3 garlic cloves, minced
1/4 tsp ground black pepper
15 oz can chickpeas, rinsed and drained
14 oz can tomatoes, diced
1 cup chicken broth
5 tsp curry powder
2 tsp ground ginger
1 bay leaf
1 tbsp vegetable oil
2 tbsp lime juice
1/2 tsp salt

- Add all ingredients into the slow cooker and mix well.
- Cover and cook on high for 4 hours.
  - Serve and enjoy.

Calories 322, Fat 11.1 g, Carbohydrates 17.4 g, Sugar 2.4 g, Protein 36.9 g, Cholesterol 101 mg

Creamy Coconut Chicken Curry

Total Time: 4 hours 15 minutes
Serves: 4

1 lb chicken breasts, skinless and boneless
2 tbsp lemon juice
1 cup green peas
1/2 tsp cayenne
2 tbsp curry powder
15 oz can tomato sauce
1/2 cup chicken stock
1/2 cup coconut milk
2 medium sweet potatoes, diced
15 oz can chickpeas, drained and rinsed
1 medium onion, sliced
1 tsp salt

- Add all ingredients except peas into the slow cooker and mix well.
- Cover and cook on high for 4 hours.
- Add peas and stir well.
- Serve and enjoy.

Calories 579, Fat 17.9 g, Carbohydrates 62.4 g, Sugar 9.5 g, Protein 44.2 g, Cholesterol 101 mg

Tasty Chicken Kheema

Total Time: 4 hours 20 minutes
Serves: 4

1 lb ground chicken
3/4 cup frozen peas
1 bay leaf
3/4 tsp ground cinnamon
3/4 tsp garam masala
3/4 tsp ground turmeric
3/4 tsp chili powder
3/4 tsp ground cumin
3/4 tsp ground coriander
1 jalapeno, seeded and chopped
4 tbsp cilantro, chopped
3/4 cup can tomato sauce
1 tsp ginger, grated
3 garlic cloves, minced
1 medium onion, chopped
2 tsp butter
1 tsp kosher salt

- Heat butter in a pan over medium heat.
- Add onion to the pan and sauté for 5 minutes.
- Add ginger and garlic and sauté for 2 minutes.
- Add ground chicken and salt and cook for 5 minutes.
- Transfer chicken mixture to the slow cooker along with remaining ingredients and stir well.
- Cover and cook on high for 4 hours.

- Serve and enjoy.

Calories 291, Fat 10.8 g, Carbohydrates 11.8 g, Sugar 4.7 g, Protein 35.8 g, Cholesterol 106 mg

Shredded Lamb

Total Time: 6 hours 15 minutes
Serves: 6

4.4 lbs lamb shoulder
3 tsp vegetable oil
1 cup chicken stock
1 tbsp ginger, sliced
4 garlic cloves, crushed
2 large onions, sliced
Spice Rub:
1 tsp red chili powder
1 tsp ground coriander
6 peppercorns
1 tsp fennel seeds
1 bay leaf
1 tsp cumin seeds
1 cinnamon stick
6 cloves
1-star anise

- Add allspice rub ingredients into the grinder and grind to coarse powder.
- Rub spice powder onto the lamb from both the sides.
- Heat oil in the pan over medium-high heat.
- Place lamb onto the pan and brown them on both the sides and set aside.
- Add remaining ingredients into the slow cooker.

- Place lamb into the slow cooker.
- Cover and cook on high for 6 hours or until meat is tender.
- Remove lamb from slow cooker and using fork shred the meat.
- Return shredded meat to the slow cooker and stir well.
- Serve with rice and enjoy.

Calories 671, Fat 27.1 g, Carbohydrates 6.7 g, Sugar 2.3 g, Protein 94.4 g, Cholesterol 299 mg

Yummy Chicken Soup

Total Time: 12 hours 15 minutes
Serves: 6

3 carrots, peeled and sliced
1 tsp ginger, crushed
1/2 tsp garlic, crushed
1/4 tsp turmeric
1/2 onion, diced
12 cups water
5 cloves
2 cinnamon sticks
1/4 tsp black peppercorns
2 chicken breasts
1 lb chicken
1 tbsp sea salt

- Add all ingredients into the slow cooker.
- Cover and cook on low for 12 hours.
- Remove chicken from slow cooker and using fork shred the chicken.
- Return shredded chicken to the slow cooker and stir well.
- Season with pepper and salt.
  - Serve and enjoy.

Calories 225, Fat 5.9 g, Carbohydrates 4.3 g, Sugar 1.9 g, Protein 36.4 g, Cholesterol 102 mg

Sweet Beef Curry

Total Time: 8 hours 15 minutes
Serves: 6

2.2 lbs stew beef
1 tbsp raisins
1 tbsp relish
1 tbsp tomato sauce
2 carrots, peeled and chopped
1 onion, chopped
2 celery stalks, chopped
2 apples, chopped
1 tbsp Worcestershire sauce
1/2 cup water
1 tbsp golden syrup
2 tbsp brown sugar
1 tbsp curry powder
2 tsp salt

- Add all ingredients into the slow cooker and mix well.
- Cover and cook on low for 8 hours.
    - Serve and enjoy.

Calories 333, Fat 10.3 g, Carbohydrates 23 g, Sugar 15.7 g, Protein 37.4 g, Cholesterol 0 mg

Yellow Chicken Curry

Total Time: 4 hours 15 minutes
Serves: 6

1 1/2 lbs chicken thighs, boneless, skinless and cut into pieces
1 lb potatoes, diced
1 medium onion, diced
13.5 oz can coconut milk
2 tbsp brown sugar
1 tsp ground turmeric
1 tsp curry powder
2 tsp garlic, minced
1 tbsp fresh ginger, minced
1/2 tsp ground coriander seed
1/2 tsp red pepper
1 tsp kosher salt

- Add all ingredients into the slow cooker and stir well.
- Cover and cook on low for 4 hours.
  - Serve and enjoy.

Calories 296, Fat 8.7 g, Carbohydrates 20.5 g, Sugar 5.1 g, Protein 35.9 g, Cholesterol 101 mg

Spinach Lamb Curry

Total Time: 4 hours 20 minutes
Serves: 8

2 cups plain yogurt
6 cups baby spinach
3 lbs lamb meat, boneless and cut into pieces
2 cups beef broth
1 1/2 tsp ground turmeric
1 1/2 tsp cayenne pepper
2 tsp ground cumin
1 tsp fresh ginger, grated
4 garlic cloves, minced
3 onions, chopped
1/3 cup vegetable oil
Salt

- Heat oil in the pan over medium-high heat.
- Add garlic and onions to the pan and sauté for 5 minutes.
- Add turmeric, cayenne, cumin, and ginger and sauté for 1 minute.
- Add broth to the pan and stir well.
- Add meat into the slow cooker with salt.
- Pour pan mixture over the meat.
- Cover and cook on high for 4 hours.
- Just before serving add spinach and cook until wilted, about 5 minutes.
- Add yogurt and stir well.
    - Serve and enjoy.

Calories 479, Fat 23 g, Carbohydrates 10.6 g, Sugar 6.4 g, Protein 53.8 g, Cholesterol 157 mg

Classic Lamb Curry

Total Time: 6 hours 15 minutes
Serves: 6

3.3 lbs lamb, diced
2 bay leaves
2 cardamom pods
1 cinnamon stick
1 cup chicken stock
1 tsp red chili powder
1 tsp paprika
1 tsp garam masala
4 tsp ground cumin
4 tsp ground coriander
1 tsp turmeric
6 garlic cloves, crushed
1 tsp ginger, grated
1 large onion, sliced
3 tbsp vegetable oil
1/4 cup all-purpose flour
Salt

- Add flour and lamb into the large zip-lock bag and shake well and set aside.

- Meanwhile, heat 2 tbsp oil in the large frying pan over high heat.
- Add lamb to the pan and cook until browned on both the sides, about 7 minutes.
- Transfer lamb into the slow cooker.
- Heat remaining oil in the pan over medium-high heat.
- Add garlic, ginger, and onion to the pan and sauté for 2 minutes.
- Add turmeric, red chili powder, paprika, garam masala, cumin, and coriander and sauté for 2 minutes.
- Add chicken stock and stir well.
- Transfer pan mixture to the slow cooker.
- Add bay leaves, cardamom, and cinnamon stick.
- Cover and cook on low for 6 hours.
  - Serve and enjoy.

Calories 568, Fat 25.7 g, Carbohydrates 8.7 g, Sugar 1.3 g, Protein 71.5 g, Cholesterol 225 mg

Easy Lamb Stew

Total Time: 4 hours 15 minutes
Serves: 4

2 lbs lamb, boneless
2 medium onions, chopped
3 garlic cloves, chopped
1 tsp fresh ginger, grated
1 tsp dried mint
2 tbsp vegetable oil
2 tsp ground cumin

2 tsp ground coriander
1 tsp ground turmeric
28 oz can tomatoes, crushed
1.5 tbsp maple syrup
1 tsp garam masala
1 tsp red chili flakes
2 tsp salt

- Heat oil in the pan over medium heat.
- Add ginger, garlic, and onion to the pan and sauté for 5 minutes.
- Add lamb and cook until browned. Transfer pan mixture into the slow cooker.
- Add remaining ingredients and stir well.
- Cover and cook on high for 4 hours.
    - Serve warm and enjoy.

Calories 577, Fat 28.8 g, Carbohydrates 22.2 g, Sugar 13.6 g, Protein 66.5 g, Cholesterol 204 mg

Spicy Beef Roast

Total Time: 5 hours 15 minutes
Serves: 6

2 1/2 lbs beef roast
25 curry leaves
1 tbsp ginger, grated
1 Serrano pepper, minced

2 tbsp lemon juice
2 tbsp garlic, minced
1 tbsp garam masala
1 tsp coriander powder
2 tsp chili powder
1 tsp turmeric
1/2 tsp black pepper
2 onions, chopped
2 tbsp coconut oil
1 tsp mustard seeds
1 tsp salt

- Add all ingredients into the slow cooker and mix well.
- Cover and cook on high for 5 hours.
    - Using fork shred the meat and serves.

Calories 421, Fat 16.8 g, Carbohydrates 6.2 g, Sugar 1.9 g, Protein 58.4 g, Cholesterol 169 mg

Spicy Beef Stew

Total Time: 8 hours 25 minutes
Serves: 4

1 lb beef stew meat
1 cup beef broth
1 onion, sliced
14.5 oz can tomatoes, diced
1 tbsp curry powder
1 fresh jalapeno pepper, diced
1 tsp fresh ginger, chopped
2 garlic cloves, minced
1 tbsp vegetable oil
Pepper
Salt

- Heat oil in the pan over medium heat.
- Add beef to the pan and cook until brown. Transfer to the slow cooker.
- Season browned beef with pepper and salt.
- In same pan, sauté ginger, garlic, and jalapeno for 2 minutes.
- Add tomatoes and curry powder and stir for a minute. Transfer pan mixture to the slow cooker.
- Add remaining ingredients and mix well.
- Cover and cook on low for 8 hours.
  - Serve and enjoy.

Calories 293, Fat 11.1 g, Carbohydrates 10 g, Sugar 5 g, Protein 37.2 g, Cholesterol 101 mg

Part 2

Indian best recipes

1. Aloo Palak

Ingredients

3 cups chopped spinach
2 large onoins chopped fine
2 large potatoes boiled and peeled 1 tomato grated
2 green chillies
1" piece ginger
1 tsp. lemon juice
1/2 tsp. wheat or other flour 1 tsp. red chilli powder
1 tsp. cinnamon-clove powder 1/4 tsp. turmeric powder
1/2 tsp cumin seeds 2 pinches asafoetida
1/2 tsp. garam masala 1/2 tbsp. butter
4 tbsp. ghee salt to taste

METHOD:

Put the washed spinach in a pan, add very little water (just a sprinkle) and a pinch of salt.
Cover and boil over a high flame for 2 minutes. Cool quickly, or hold under running water in a colander. Put in a mixie, add green chilli and run for a minute. Keep slightly coarse, do not make very smooth.
Keep aside.

Cut the potatoes into big pieces. Heat ghee and fry potatoes till light brown. Drain the potatoes, keep aside.
In the same hot ghee add the cumin seeds. Add the ginger, onions and fry till very tender.
Add the tomato and further fry for two minutes. Add all the dry masalas and fry till ghee separates. Add spinach and potatoes.

When it resumes a boil sprinkle the flour and stir well. Boil for 2-3 minutes. Add lemon juice Just before serving heat butter in a tiny saucepan and add the asafoetida.
Pour over the vegetable and mix gently. Serve hot with naan or parathas or even rice.
Note: You may use boiled peas, boiled corn kernels or paneer chunks in the above dish, instead of atoes. Making time: 45 minutes
Makes for: 6
Shelf life: Best fresh

2. Gobi Manchurian

INGREDIENTS:

1 medium. cauliflower clean and broken into big florettes.

1 small bunch spring onoin finely chopped 2 tsp. ginger finely chopped
1 tsp. garlic finely chopped 1/4 cup plain flour
3 tbsp. cornflour
1/4 tsp. red chilli powder 2 red chillies, dry
3 tbsp. oil
1 1/2 cups water 1 tbsp. milk

METHOD:

Boil the florettes for 3-4 minutes in plenty of water, to which a tbsp. of milk has been added. Drain and pat dry on a clean cloth.

Make thin batter out of flour and 2 tbsp.cornflour, adding 1/4 tsp. each of ginger and garlic and red chilli powder and salt to taste.
Dip the florettes in the batter one by one and deep fry in hot oil. Keep aside.

In the remaining oil, add remaining ginger, garlic and crushed red chilli and fry for a minute. Add the salt and spring onions. Stir fry for a minute. Add 1 1/2 cups water and bring to a boil. Add 1 tbsp. cornflour to 1/4 cup water and dissolve well. Gradually add to the gravy and stir continuously till it resumes boiling. Boil till the gravy becomes transparent. Add florettes and soya sauce. Boil for two more minutes and remove.
Serve hot with noodles or rice.

Variations:

Dry manchurian can be made by omitting the gravy.
Make florettes as above and instead of adding water as above, add fried florettes, spring onions and soya ce at this stage. Sprinkle 1 tsp. cornflour on the florettes and stirfry for 2 minutes.
Serve piping hot with toothpicks or miniforks and chilligarlic sauce or tomato sauce.
Same procedure for veg. manchurian (with gravy or dry), but instead of using only cauliflower, use finely chopped minced vegetables and
bind with some cornflour or bread crumbs and make small lumps the size of a pingpong ball. Fry as above and proceed as above.

Making time: 45 minutes Makes for: 6
Shelf life: Best fresh

3. Sindhi Saibhaji

Ingredients:

1 each - carrot, capsicum, onion, small cabbage, potato, brinjal, tomato, ladyfinger (okra) 100 gms. french beans
1/2 bunch each spinach, coriander, khatta (3 leaved) greens.
1/2 bunch any other leafy greens. 1 cup green gram dal
1/2 cup horsegram dal (channa dal) 4-5 green chillies
2-3 clovettes garlic
1 tsp. red chilli powder
1 tsp. dhania (coriander seed) powder 1 tsp. salt
1/2 tsp. turmeric 3 tbsp. oil
1/2 tbsp. ghee
2 pinches asafoetida METHOD:
Clean and wash dals.
Clean, wash and chop spinach and vegetables except tomato. Heat oil in a pressure cooker, add all the vegetables, spinach and dals. Mix well, add enough water to cover the contents.

Add all masalas and mix.
Place whole tomato on top, cover and pressurecook for 3 whistles. Cool the cooker, open and handblend the contents. Heat 1/2 tbsp. ghee add a pinch of asafoetida add to the mashed vegetable. Serve hot with paratha or steamed rice

Making time: 30 minutes (excluding cooling time) Makes for: 6
Shelf life: Best fresh

4. Shahi Paneer

Ingredients:

250 gms. paneer (cottge cheese) 3 tbsp. ghee or butter
1 onion chopped into strips 1/2" piece ginger chopped fine 2 green chillies chopped fine 4 tomatoes chopped fine
2 cardamoms crushed 1/4 cup beaten curd
1/2 tsp. red chilli powder 1/2 tsp. garam masala salt to taste
1/2 cup milk
2 tbsp. tomato sauce

To garnish:
2 tbsp. grated paneer
1 tbsp. chopped coriander Method:
Chop the paneer into 2" fingers.
Heat half the ghee. Add onion,ginger, green chilli and cardamom. Fry for 3-4 minutes. Add tomatoes and cook for 7-8 minutes, covered.
Add curd and cook for 5 minutes. Add 1/2 cup water and cool.
Blend in a mixie till smooth.

Heat remaining ghee, add gravy and other ingredients except milk and paneer. Boil to get a very thick gravy.
Just before serving, heat gravy, add milk and paneer fingers and boil for 3-4 minutes. Garnish with chopped coriander and grated paneer.

Making time: 45 minutes.
Makes for: 6
Shelf life: best fresh.

5. Potato in Curd Gravy

Ingredients:

3 medium. potatoes boiled and peeled 1 cup curd or yogurt beaten
1 tsp. red chilli powder 1 tsp. salt
1/2 tsp. dhania powder 1/4 tsp. turmeric powder 1/4 tsp. garam masala
2 pinches asafoetida 1 stalk curry leaves
1 tbsp. coriander leaves chopped

1 1/4 cup water
1/2 tsp. each ginger, garlic grated 2 green chillies slit
1 tsp. each cumin, mustard seeds 1/4 tsp. wheat flour
1 tbsp. oil Method:
Cut potatoes into big pieces. Mash 3-4 pieces fine with hand. Keep both aside. Mix all the dry masala in 1/4 cup water. Heat oil. Add the seeds (cumin and mustard). When they splutter, add ginger-garlic, chilli and curry leaves. Add the masala mixture and fry for 2 minutes.
Add beaten curd and fry for 5 minutes or till the curd loses its whiteness. Stir continuously after adding curd.

Add the remaining water and all the potato and flour. Stir well. Boil and simmer for 10 minutes or till gravy thickens Garnish with chopped coriander.
Serve hot with thin wheat chappaties and rice.

Making time: 30 minutes.
Makes for: 5
Shelf life: Best fresh

6. Navratan Korma

Ingredients:

2 cups peas boiled
1 large carrot chopped and boiled 1/2 cup tomato sauce
1/4 cup curd
1/4 cup malai(cream) 3 tbsp. butter
1 small sweet lime 1 small apple
1 banana
2 slices pineapple
10-15 cashewnuts
20 raisins
2 glaced cherries for decoration 1 tbsp. coriander chopped
1 tbsp. ghee salt to taste

Dry Masala:
1 tsp. cuminseeds
2 tsp. khuskhus (poppyseeds) 1 tsp. cardamoms

Wet Masala:
1 large onion
1/4 cup coconut shredded 3 green chillies

Method:

Grind the dry and wet masalas separately.

Chop all the fruit fine. Heat ghee and fry cashews, drain and keep aside. Add butter to ghee and heat, add the wet masala and fry for 2 minutes. Add the dry masala and salt and fry 2 more minutes.

Add the carrots and peas, mix together curd and cream and add to gravy.

Allow to thicken a bit, add fruit, cashews and raisins and boil till the gravy is thick and the fat separates. Garnish with grated cheese ,coriander and chopped cherries.

Serve hot with naan, roti or paratha.

Making time: 45 minutes Makes for: 6
Shelf life: Best fresh

7. Malai Kofta

Ingredients:

Gravy:
125 gms. cream
75 gms. khoya or paneer 150 ml. milk
50 gms. cashewnuts
3 tsp. white pepper powder.
2 1/2 tsp. sugar
2 tsp. grated ginger
1/4 tsp. nutmeg powder 1/2 tsp. turmeric powder 1 tsp. garlic crushed
1" cinnamon
6 cloves
6 cardamoms salt to taste

3 tbsp. ghee
Kofta:

50 gms. khoya
50 gms. paneer
5 medium potatoes
20 gms. cashewnuts
20 gms. raisins
4-5 green chillies chopped fine 1/2 tsp. ginger grated
1 tsp. coriander chopped 1/2 tsp. cumin seeds
salt to taste Garnish:
1 tbsp. grated cheese or paneer 1 tbsp. chopped coriander

Method:
Koftas
Boil the potatoes, peel and smash them.
Mix together all the ingredients except raisins and cashews.
Take a ping-pong ball sized dough in hand.
Flatten. Place 2-3 cashews and raisins in the centre and shape into a ball. Repeat for remaining dough. Keep aside.

Gravy:
Roast the cinnamon, cardamom, nutmeg and cloves together. Dry grind and keep aside. Wet grind all the other ingredients, except ghee, to a paste. Heat ghee in a skillet, add powdered spices and fry for 2-3 seconds.
Add paste and fry further for 5-7 minutes stirring well. Add 2 cups water and simmer on low for 15 minutes. Warm the koftas either in the oven or on the tava.
Optional: You can deep fry the koftas also. To serve place warm koftas in a casserole.
Either pour boiling hot gravy on the koftas or pour and bake in hot oven of 5 minutes. Garnish with grated cheese and chopped coriander.
Serve hot with naan or parathas.

Making time: 45 minutes. Makes: 10 koftas with gravy. Shelf life: Best fresh.

8. Samosa

Ingredients For cover:
1 cup plain flour (maida) 2 tbsp. warm oil
water to knead dough

For filling:
2 potatoes large boiled, peeled, mashed 1 onion finely chopped

2 green chillies crushed 1/2 tsp. ginger crushed 1/2 tsp. garlic crushed
1 tbsp. coriander finely chopped 1/2 lemon juice extracted
1/2 tsp. turmeric powder 1/2 tsp. garam masala
1/2 tsp. coriander seeds crushed 1 tsp. red chilli powder
salt to taste oil to deep fry

Method For dough:
Make well in the flour.
Add oil, salt and little water.Mix well till crumbly.
Add more water little by little, kneading into soft pliable dough. Cover with moist cloth, keep aside for 15-20 minutes. Beat dough on worksurface and knead again. Re-cover.

For filling:
Heat 3 tbsp. oil, add ginger, green chilli, garlic, coriander seeds. Stir fry for a minute, add onion, saute till light brown. Add coriander, lemon, turmeric, salt, red chilli, garam masala. Stir fry for 2 minutes, add potatoes. Stir further 2 minutes.

Cool. Keep aside.

To proceed:
Make a thin 5" diam. round with some dough.
Cut into two halves. Run a moist finger along diameter. Join and press together to make a cone.
Place a tbsp. of filling in the cone and seal third side as above. Make five to six. Put in hot oil, deep fry on low to medium till light brown. Do not fry on high, or the samosas will turn out oily and soggy.
Drain on rack or kitchen paper.
Serve hot with green and tamarind chutneys (refer chutneys), or tomato sauce.

Making time: 45 minutes Makes: 20 pieces (approx.) Shelflife: Bestfresh

9. Masala Vada

Ingredients

1 cup yellow gram (chana) dak 1/2 cup onion finely chopped
1/2 cup coriander finely chopped
1/2 cup dill leaves finely chopped 3-4 green chillies finely chopped 1/2 tsp. cumin seeds
oil o deep fry Method
Wash and soak dal for 3-4 hours.
Keep 2 tbsp. dal aside, grind the rest,coarsely. Mix all other ingredients, including whole dal. Add 2-3 tbsp. hot oil to the mixture.
Heat oil, make pattie shaped rounds with moist palm. Let carefully into the hot oil.
Fry first one side then the other till golden brown.
Serve hot with green chutney, tamarind chutney, or ketchup

Making time: 20 minutes (excluding soaking time) Makes: 15 vadas (approx.)
Shelflife: Best fresh

10. Hot Kachori

Ingredients For cover:
1 1/2 cup plain flour 3 tbsp. oil
salt to taste
cold water to knead dough

For filling:
1 cup yellow moong dal washed and soaked for 1/2 hour 1 tsp. garam masala
1 tsp. red chilli powder
1/2 tsp. dhania (coriander) powder
1/2 tsp. coriander seeds crushed coarsely
1/2 tsp. fennel (saunf) seeds crushed coarsely 1/2 tsp. cumin seeds
1/2 tsp. mustard seeds
1 tbsp. coriander leaves finely chopped salt to taste
2-3 pinches asafoetida
1 tbsp. oil
oil to deep fry
1 tbsp. plain flour for patching Method
For cover:
Mix flour, salt and oil, knead into soft pliable dough. Keep aside for 30 minutes.

For filling:
Put plenty of water to boil. Add dal. Boil dal for 5 minutes, drain.

Cool a little. Heat oil in a heavy pan.
Add all seeds whole and crushed allow to splutter. Add asafoetida, mix. Add all other ingredients.
Mix well. Do not smash the dal fully.
But enough to make the mixture hold well. Remove from fire, cool.
Divide into 15 portions.

Shape into balls with greased palms. Keep aside.

To proceed:
Make a paste with water, of flour for patching. Keep aside.
Take a pingpong ball sized portion of dough. Knead into round. Roll into 4" diam. round. Place one ball of filling at centre.
Pick up round and wrap ball into it like a pouch. Break off excess dough carefully.
Do not allow cover to tear.
Press the ball with palm, making it flattish and round. Repeat for 4-5 kachories.
Deep fry in hot oil, on low flame only.
If the kachori get a hole anywhere, apply some paste. Return to oil and finish frying.
Turn and repeat for other side.
Fry till golden and crisp. Small bubbles must appear over kachori. Drain and serve hot with green and tamarind chutneys.

Making time: 1 hour (excluding soaking and cooling times)
Makes: 10-12 pieces
Shelf life: 2-3 days

Note: Take care to fry on low. Hurried frying will result in soggy and oily kachories.

11. Spicy Sev

Ingredients

2 cups gram flour (besan) 1/2 tsp. ajwain (omam) seeds 1 1/2 tsp. red chilli powder
1 tbsp. oil salt to taste
2-3 pinches asafoetida water to make dough oil to deep fry

Method

1. Mix the chilli, oil, salt and seeds into the flour.
2. Add enough water to make a dough which is quite gooey.
3. It should not be pliable but sticky.
4. Grease the inside of a Sev-press, fill with the dough. 5.Press into hot oil, and fry lightly on both sides.
6. Drain well and cool before storing. Variation:
You may adjust the chillies as per taste.

You may omit chillies to make bland sev.
You may add finely crushed dried herbs (eg. mint) for add flavour.
Note: A sevpress is similar to a vermicelli press, but it should be small enough to handle over hot oil. Making time: 15-20 minutes
Makes: 250 grams approx.

12. Pear and Mango Chutney

Ingredients:

250 gms. raw firm mango 250 gms. pears.
500 gms. sugar
2 tsp. salt
1 tsp. red chilli powder 1 tsp. garam masala
1 tbsp. marshmelon (kharbooja) seeds. 1 tbsp. raisins.
2 cloves powdered
8 each almonds and cashews chopped finely. Method:
Peel and mash and pear.
Put 1 tbsp. sugar in a heavy saucepan.
Heat on a low flame, stirring and cooking till it turns brown.
Add 500 ml. water and boil.
When the sugar has fully dissolved in the water add remaining sugar.
When it begins to boil again add the mashed fruit, cashew, raisins, seeds, chilli and salt. Boil till a thick jam consistency is obtained. Stir occasionally.
Add the clove powder and garam masala. Cool a bit and transfer to clean airtight jar.

Making time: 1 hour Shelf life: 1 month Makes 1.5 kgs. chutney.

13. Green All-Purpose Chutney

Ingredients:

15 green chillies 1/2 cup coriander 1/2 lemon

1 tbsp. sev or potato wafers crushed
1/2 tsp. jaggery salt to taste
1 tsp. oil
1 clovette garlic Method:
Put all the ingredients, except oil and asafoetida, in a small mixie. Heat the oil and add the asafoetida and put in the mixie.
Run the mixie till a smooth chutney is obtained.
Try using no water or as little as possible to make the chutney keep longer. Add water as and when required.
Store in a clean glass bottle.
Note: Sev is a fried Indian snack made of gramflour. Makes 1/2 cup chutney
Making time: 5 minutes
Shelf life: 1 week (refrigerated)

14. Sarson ka saag

Ingredients

1 bunch sarson greens 1 bunch spinach
1 onion grated
1/2 tsp. each ginger & garlic grated 3 green chillies
1 tbsp. grated cheese or paneer (optional) 1/2 lemon juice salt to taste 2 tbsp. ghee
1 tbsp. oil
1/2 tsp. garam masala 1 tbsp. maize flour

Method

1. Chop both greens, wash, drain. 2.Heat oil in the pressure cooker direct. 3.Add both greens, green chillies, stir. 4.Add ginger, garlic, stir.
5.Add few pinches salt, 1 cup water. 6.Pressure cook till done. (2 whistles). 7.Mash well.
8.Heat ghee in a pan, add onion, saute till brown, 9.Add all other ingredients, except cheese.
10.Stir well and cook till oil separates. 11.Garnish with cheese.
12.Serve hot with makki ki roti, or paratha.
Making time: 25 minutes (excluding pressure cooking time)
Makes: 3-4 servings
Shelflife: Best fresh

15.Sweet Pongal

Ingredients (for two people) :- Moong dhal - 1/2 cup.
Rice- 1/2 cup.
Milk
Coconut cashew jaggery
raisins (khish-mish - dry grapes) cardamom
ghee.

Fry the moong dhal (before washing) till it becomes little light brown (it will start smelling). Then soak rice and dhal separately for 10 minutes. Thoroghly wash and keep it in cooker with the right water (lesser is o.k)and cook it seperately (in two different containers). Meanwhile cut coconut in very small pieces and fry in ghee. Fry cashew and raisins also separately.
Break the jagerry and put in water (very little) and make a syrup. This is

done because sometimes jagerry has mud and stones. After we make the syrup strain it through tea strainer. Put the rice and dhal in a big vessel and
add milk (may be one cup) and cook it till all the milk gets absorbed. Add jaggery syrup and again cook till even it gets absorbed. Add three big table spoons of ghee, powdered cardamon and cook again for a while. Add fried coconut, cashews and raisins.

Serve hot in two cups with a spoon of ghee.

16.Ulundu vada

urad dhaal hari mirch salt

Soak dhaal in water over night. Grind dhaal in little water. Then make vada shape and deep fry in oil.

17.Adai

Rice - ½ cup
urad dhaal - ¼ cup chana dhaal - ¼ cup thoor dhaal - ¼ cup yellow moong dhaal - ¼ cup red chillis
salt

Soak everything in water over night. Grind with little water.

18.Dhaal vada

urad dhaal - chana dhaal - red chillis -

Following is the thread test (tar) to check required consistency of syrup (chashni). If no thread is formed, but there is stickiness in the syrup when tested, then it is 3/4 tar (thread). This consistency is generally used in dipping sweets like, gulabjamoon, boondi, jalebi, imarti, etc. Boil some more and when 1 tar forms, it is used in soaking pancake pancakes like malpua. On further boiling two tars are obtained and this is used in sweets like burfis, mohanthal, etc. At this stage a drop of syrup dropped on a plate will form a soft ball when cooled. After this stage do no stir briskly and continuously or the sugar will recrystallise. Still further boiling will form 2 1/2 to 3 tars and this syrup is used to get a white coating of sugar on sweets like balushahi, surti ghari, etc. At this stage when the syrup is dropped in a plate it will form a hard ball when cooled. Following are the steps shown to make sugar syrup (chashni) in the right way.

a. Take sugar and water in the ratio of 2 : 1 1/2 unless other wise mentioned. b. Put both in a deep saucepan to boil, stirring occasionally.
c. When the mixture comes to a boil, add 1/2 cup milk.
d. When a thick scum is formed on the surface of syrup, it is time to strain. e. Always use a metal strainer or moist cloth to strain the hot syrup, never plastic. f. Put back to boil, checking the consistency required as above.
g. Check frequently, because once the first thread forms, it proceeds to thicken to the next stages very quickly. h. Use as required in the recipe. Make syrup side by side of making the recipe, reheating the syrup too many times will alter the texture of the resulting sweet dish. To save time, prepare the syrup on a second burner, while making the rest of the recipe. This will avoid excess wastage of time and unnecessary cooling off, of the fried flours, etc. as the recipe demands.

19. Shrikhand

Ingredients 1/2 kg. curds
300 gms. sugar
1/2 tsp. cardamom powder few strands saffron
1/2 tbsp. pista & almond crushed Method
Tie curd in a clean muslin cloth overnight. (6-7 hours). Take into a bowl, add sugar and mix.
Keep aside for 25-30 minutes to allow sugar to dissolve.
Rub saffron into 1 tbsp. milk till well broken and dissolved. Keep aside. Beat well till sugar has fully dissolved into curd. Pass through a big holed strong strainer, pressing with hand or spatula. Mix in cardamom powder and dissolved saffron and half nuts.
Empty into a glass serving bowl, top with remaining nut crush. Chill for 1-2 hours before serving.

Making time: 20 minutes (excluding tieing and keeping time)
Makes: 6-7 servings
Shelflife: 3-4 days refrigerated

Variations: To make fruit flavoured shrikhand eg. mango, add pulp at the stage of adding cardamom and saffron.

20. Puranpoli

Ingredients

300gms. channa (yellowgram) dal 300 gms. jaggery (molasses)
1 tsp. cardamom powder 150 gms. plain flour
1 tbsp. ghee
warm water to knead dough ghee to serve

Method

Boil dal in plenty of water till soft but not broken. Drain in a colander for 10-15 minutes.
Pass through an almond grater little by little till all dal is grated. Mash jaggery till lumps break. Mix well into dal.
Put mixture in a heavy saucepan and cook till a soft lump is formed Take care to stir continuously, so as not to charr. Keep aside.
Mix ghee, flour, add enough water to make a soft pliable dough. Take a morsel sized ball of dough, roll into a 4" round. Place same sized ball of filling in centre, life all round and seal. Reroll carefully to a 6" diameter round.
Roast on warm griddle till golden brown. Repeat other side. Take on serving plate. Apply a tsp. of ghee all over top. OR Shallow fry on griddle like a paratha for a better flavour. But this method will consume more ghee and therefore calories. Serve hot with dal or amti.

Note: The water drained from boiling dal is used to make the amti. (a thin curry made using black masala, garam masala and some mashed
dal.)

Making time: 45 minutes Makes: 7-8 puranpolis
Shelflife: Best fresh (puran {filling} may be stored in the refrigerator for a week.

21. Patisa (Soan Papdi)

Ingredients

1 1/4 cup gramflour
1 1/4 cup plain flour (maida) 250 gms. ghee
2 1/2 cups sugar 1 1/2 cup water 2 tbsp. milk
1/2 tsp. cardamom seeds crushed coarsely
2 tsp. charmagaz (combination of 4 types of seeds) refer glossary 4" squares cut from a thin polythene sheet

Method

Sift both flours together.
Heat ghee in a heavy saucepan.
Add flour mixture and roast on low till light golden. Keep aside to cool a little, stirring occasionally.
Prepare syrup simultaneously.
Make syrup out of sugar, water and milk as shown in introduction. Bring syrup to 2 1/2 thread consistency.
Pour at once into the flour mixture.
Beat well with a large fork till the mixture forms threadlike flakes. Pour onto a greased surface or thali and roll to 1" thickness lightly.
Sprinkle the charmagaz seeds and elaichi and gently press down with palm.
Cool, cut into 1" squares, wrap individually into square pieces of thin plastic sheet. Store in airtight container.

Making time: 45 minutes Makes: 20 pieces (approx.) Shelflife: 2 weeks

22. Coconut Burfi

Ingredients

250 gms. finely grated coconut 250 gms. sugar
150 ml. water
ghee for greasing plate Method
1. Prepare syrup with sugar and water to 2 1/2 thread consistency. Use method as shown in introduction.
2. Warm coconut in heavy saucepan, pour in the syrup.
3. Stir well and cook till soft lump forms.
4. Spread in a greased plate. Cool.
5. Sprinkle cardamom powder (optional). 6. Cut into squares, store in airtight container.

Making time: 30 minutes Makes: 20-25 pieces
Shelflife: 2 weeks

23. Imarti

Ingredients

2 cups urad dal 3 cups sugar
300 ml. water saffron colour
1/2 tsp. cardomom ground 500 gms. ghee to fry

Method

1. Soak urad dal overnight in plenty of water.
2. Wash and drain. Grind to fine thick batter. Put water little by little. 3.Add colour and mix very well.
4.If using a mixie, beat the dal well by hand till fluffy after grinding. 5.Keep aside for 3 hours. More is weather is cold. 6.Make 1 tar sugar syrup as shown in introduction. 7.Add cardomom powder to syrup.
8. Using either an imarti bottle (with nozzle) or cloth as shown in note, form imartis in the hot ghee.
Lower flame and allow to crisp turning once.
9. Remove from ghee, drain and dip in hot syrup. 10.Soak for 3-4 minutes, drain and serve.
11. Repeat for remaining batter.
12. Make 4-5 imartis at a time, depending on size of frying pan. Note:
Use a flat bottomed frying pan.
The imarti bottle can be substituted with a soft plastic sauce bottle with a nozzle. If not available, take a 12"x 12" thick cloth, make a buttonhole type hole in centre. Place over a tumbler and pour in some batter.
Hold like a pouch and press out imartis like icing.
Shape the imartis as follows, make a ring first, then form small ringlets all along the ring. Till you come to the start.

Making time: 1 hour (excluding soaking and keeping time)
Makes: 20 imartis
Shelflife: (1) Keep unsoaked in syrup for a day. (2) Soak in syrup as required.

24.Kaju Barfi

150 gm cashewnuts
400 gm sugar elaichi powdered silver foil (optional) 500 gm khoya

Method

Dry grind the cashew
Mix khoya (grated) and sugar
Heat in a heavy pan, stirring continuously.
Once the sugar dissolves, add the cashew (powdered) and elaichi Cooking, constantly stir till soft lump is formed and does not stick to sides Roll on a flat surface to desired thickness and apply silver foil.

25. Khajur Burfi or Rolls

1 tin condensed milk
1 kg khajur deseeded (dates)
250 gm mixed dryfruits (badam, cashew, pista) 1/2 cup dessicated dry coconut

Method

Break up khajur coarsely
Add milkmaid and dryfruit all in a heavy, non-stick pan. Cook on slow flame, stirring continuously.
Do not allow to stick to bottom. It takes a while to cook
Stir gently till a soft lump forms.
Spread some of the coconut on a butter paper sheet.
Grease hands and take a chunk of the mixture and roll into a thick roll, on the sheet, all the coconut to cover it.
Chill the rolls in the fridge Cut into slices

Or set in a tray and cut into squares.

26. Kalakand (Milk Burfi)

2 litres milk
1/2 to 3/4 cup sugar
chopped nuts to decorate (pista, almonds) silver foil (optional)
1/2 tsp citric acid dissolved in 1/2 cup water.

Method

Boil half the milk and add the citric solution as it comes to boil
Switch off gas. Once the chenna settles sieve through muslin cloth, press out excess water, take in a plate and press down. Do not knead.
Put the remaining milk in a heavy pan and boil to half.
Add the chenna and boil till the mixture thickens, stirring continuously.
Add the sugar and continue to cook, stirring all the while till softly thickens in a lump. Set in a tray, apply silver foil and sprinkle the chopped nuts.

27. Badam ka seera

1 1/2 cup almonds soaked overnight 3 cups hot milk

250 gm ghee
1/2 to 1/3 cup sugar Method
Peel the almonds, wash and grind to fine paste. Heat ghee in a heavy pan.
Add paste and cook on first high then slow flame, stirring continuosly. After a while it should turn a light brown and aromatic.
Carefully pour hot milk and stir.
Use a long-handled spatula as the mixture tends to splatter. When thickens, add the sugar and cook, stirring continously and gently till ghee begins to separate. Decorate with chopped nuts and serve hot.

28. Carrot Halwa

1 kg juicy orange carrots 1 1/2 litre milk
400-500 gm sugar
elaichi powder (cardomon) saffron few flakes
few drops orange colour (optional) 1 tbsp ghee

Method

Peel and grate carrots
Put milk and carrots in a heavy saucepan. Boil till thick, stirring occassionally. Once it starts thickening, stir continuously. Add sugar and cook
further till thickens. Add ghee, elaichi, saffron and colour. Stir on low heat till the mixture collects in a soft ball or the ghee oozes out. Serve
hot, decorated with a chopped almond or pista.

29. Doodhi Halwa

1 kg doodhi
1 1/2 litre milk 400-500 gm sugar
elaichi powder (cardomon) saffron few flakes
1 tbsp ghee Method
Peel and grate Dudhi
Put milk and dudhi in a heavy saucepan. Boil till thick, stirring occassionally. Once it starts thickening, stir continuously. Add sugar and cook
further till thickens. Add ghee, elaichi, saffron and colour. Stir on low heat till the mixture collects in a soft ball or the ghee oozes out. Serve
hot, decorated with a chopped almond or pista.

30. Chickoo Halwa

6 chickoos
1/2 tea cup milk 1/4 - 1/3 cup sugar
150 gms khoya or milk powder made paste. 2 - 3 drops cochineal (essence)
1 tbsp ghee Method
Peel and mash chickoos or blend. Add milk and boil in heavy saucepan.
When slightly thick add khoya and cook, stirring continuously.

Add sugar and ghee. Cook on low turning continuously till ghee oozes. Garnish with almond or walnut in centre of the halwa.

31. Dal ka seera

500 gm Moong dal (green) 500 gm sugar
500 gm ghee
saffron soaked in a little milk elaichi powder

water about 250 ml. Method
Soak the dal for 5-6 hours.
Wash and remove the skins well.
Grind dal fine either in a stone grinder or electric grinder or mixie. Use as little water as possible.
Put sugar and water in a pan and put to boil. Once sugar dissolve add a few tblsp. of milk. As the syrup boils the scum will rise.
Remove with a strain.
Further boil till the syrup become sticky between the fingers. (One thread should fall when poured from a tilted spoon) keep aside. Heat the ghee in a heavy kadai (vessel) and add dal.
Keep stirring rigorously to avoid burning.
Once the dal stops sticking to the vessel, stir gradually till golden brown, and ghee begins to separate. Pour the hot syrup, add elaichi and dissolved saffron.

Stir very carefully, not allowing hand to be scalded. Cook slowly till all water is absorbed. Decorate with chopped dry fruit.

Serve hot especially on a cold day.

32. Atte ka seera

2 tbsp. wheat flour 2 1/2 tbsp. ghee
3/4 to 1 cup sugar or molasses (jaggery) elaichi powder chopped pista and almonds Method
Add flour and roast on slow fire, stirring continuously Side by side add to sugar 2 1/2 cups water and keep to boil
When the atta becomes a golden brown, add the boiling sweet water
Stir gently and continuously till excess water evaporates and the ghee separates. Decorate with chopped nuts

33. Beetroot Halwa

1 kg beetroot 1 1/2 litre milk
400-500 gm sugar
elaichi powder (cardomon) saffron few flakes
1 tbsp ghee Method

Peel and grate beetroot

Put milk and dudhi in a heavy saucepan. Boil till thick, stirring occassionally. Once it starts thickening, stir continuously. Add sugar and cook
further till thickens. Add ghee, elaichi, saffron and colour. Stir on low heat till the mixture collects in a soft ball or the ghee oozes out. Serve
hot, decorated with a chopped almond or pista.

34. Rava (Semolina) Ladoo

Ingredients:

1 cup rava 3/4 cup sugar 2 tbsp. ghee 1/4 cup milk

METHOD:

Take ghee in a deep saucepan and heat.
Add rava and cook on low heat. Stir continuously.
When the rava turns light brown add the sugar. Stir for 3-4 minutes.
Keep aside cool for some time. Add cardomom powder, coconut flakes and saffron. Add half the milk. Mix well. Wet hand with milk and shape the mixture in ladoos.

Serves: 12 helpings Time required: 1/2 hr. Shelf life : 15 days

35. Rossogolla

Ingredients:

1 litre milk
1/2 tsp. citric acid 1 1/2 cups sugar 4 cups water
2-3 drops rose essence Method:
Heat the milk and bring to boil.
Cool the milk for a couple of hours. Remove the cream layer. Reheat the milk and bring to a boil.
Add the citric acid dissolved in some water. Stir slowly till the milk is fully curdled.
Keep as it is for 5 minutes.
Meanwhile heat the sugar and water in a wide sauce pan. Bring to a boil.
Strain the milk through a muslin cloth. Wash the chenna in the cloth under cold running water. Press out the excess water and remove in a wide plate.
Gently knead into a soft dough by passing between fingers. Make twelve equal sized balls of the dough.
Let them into the boiling water. Cover with a perforated lid. Boil for 13 to 15 minutes. Take off from heat and cool them to room temperature.
Add essence and chill for at least 4 to 5 hours.

Serves: 6 helpings
Time required: 1/2 hour.

36. Pedhas

INGREDIENTS

500 gms. khoya (mawa) 300 gms. sugar
3 drops colour as required 8 to 10 pistas sliced
1/2 tsp. cardamom powder cookie mould

Method:

Grate khoya . Powder sugar . Mix together in a skillet . Heat on low flame , stiring continously .
Cook till mixture thickens . It should form a very soft lump .
Cool for 10 minutes . Add cardamom powder & colour . Mix well .
Take a small fistful of mixture . Form a ball . Press into the cookie mould . Turn out carefully . Press 2-3 slices of pista on the centre .
Repeat for remaining mixture .

Note on khoya.
Khoya is available in most Indian sweetmeat stores anywhere. Making at home consumes time but isn't that difficult.
Boil milk on high flame in a large heavy saucepan till water evaporates , leaving a soft lump. Stir frequently while cooking.
OR Substitute with 1 tin (400 gms.) condensed milk and 1 cup milk.
Lessen sugar by 1/2. Boil till a soft lump is formed. Stir continuously while cooking.

Serves: 36 pieces Time required: 1/2 hr.
Shelf Life: 15 days(refrigerated)

37.Mava Burfi

Ingredients:

500 gms khoya

300 gms. powdered sugar 1 tsp. cardamom powder
2 sheets silver foil (edible)

Method:

Mash khoya . Mix in tne sugar. Put into a heavy saucepan. Cook on slow flame, stirring continuously.
Cook till the mixture is a very soft lump.*

Place on a working board and roll with a rolling pin to 1/2 inch thickness. Cool a little. Spread on the working board silver foil carefully and evenly. Make incisions with knife to cut in the desired size and shape.
Note: Burfi is usually cut into 1 1/2 inch squares. Variation: To make chocolate mava burfi: Follow till * as above. Divide the mixture in two parts 1/3 and 2/3 In the smaller part mix 1 tablespoon cocoa powder and 1/2 tsp. chocolate colour. Roll both parts separately. Place the chocolate on the mava layer. Roll lightly. Continue as for mavaburfee.

Serves: 25 helpings Time required:1/2 hr. Shelf life: 10 days

38. Malai Ladoo

Ingredients

1/2 cup condensed milk
250 gms. paneer (cottage cheese) 2-3 drops kewra essence
1/4 tsp. yellow colour Method
1. Mash paneer.
2. Add condensed milk and cook on slow flame, stirring continuously. 3.Cook till thick and sides leave.

4.Add essence and remove from flame. 5.Mix well.
6. Pour on plate.
7. Cool. Make ladoos.
8. Sprinkle powdered elaichi and decorate.

www.ingramcontent.com/pod-product-compliance
Lightning Source LLC
Chambersburg PA
CBHW071831080526
44589CB00012B/975